Kathy,
I thank you
always m...
my day bet...

SOMEONE'S
SON

Rejoice

Brenda Rhodes

4/19

A MOTHER'S FIGHT FOR HER
GAY, DRUG ADDICTED SON

SOMEONE'S SON

A TRUE STORY

BRENDA RHODES

WinePressPublishing
Your Book, Defined. Since 1991.

WinePress Publishing (PO Box 428, Enumclaw, WA 98022) functions only as book publisher. As such, the ultimate design, content, editorial accuracy, and views expressed or implied in this work are those of the author.

Unless otherwise indicated, all Scripture quotations are taken from the *Holy Bible, New Living Translation*, copyright 1996, 2004. Used by permission of Tyndale House Publishers, Inc., Wheaton, Illinois 60189. All rights reserved.

Scripture references marked NIV are taken from the *Holy Bible, New International Version*®, *NIV*®. Copyright © 1973, 1978, 1984 by Biblica, Inc.™ Used by permission of Zondervan. All rights reserved worldwide. WWW.ZONDERVAN.COM

ISBN 13: 978-1-60615-017-7
ISBN 10: 1-60615-017-0
Library of Congress Catalog Card Number: 2009930078

Love never gives up, never loses faith, is always hopeful,
and endures through every circumstance.

—1 Corinthians 13:7

To my children: Ronal Paul, who lost his way in this world, but not his way to heaven, and Wendi, who always encourages me with her wit and wisdom.

Author's Note

Dear Reader,

I am honored that you have chosen to read this book, but please understand that it is not a "how to" book. It is a true story written by an ordinary mother who makes mistakes. In fact, in many cases it is a "how *not* to" book. It is honest, real, and sometimes even embarrassing, but if it touches your heart, to God be the glory.

During the eight-year struggle of my son's destructive behavior, I prayed that he would turn back to God and be completely healed. I hoped that we would eventually minister to others by sharing our testimonies with people going through similar situations. He would minister to those trapped in behaviors similar to his own, and I would speak into the lives of their families and friends. In my hopes and prayers, I envisioned a mother/son team for God.

I believe God has answered that prayer with this book. I hope you will agree.

Rejoice Always,
Brenda Rhodes

Contents

Acknowledgments

To Mary DeMuth, my God-given ghostwriter: Mary, you were my fleece. When you said you would ask God for his leading in helping me with this book, I felt confident that I had heard his voice telling me to tell my story. The moment you agreed that we would work together, I received confirmation of God's guidance and his desire to get this story told. You are a beautiful vessel of the Lord's love and compassion for others. I am so thankful for your tender heart that truly listens to our Savior. God blessed me with a brilliant, surrendered author who shares my life goal of bringing glory to God in our trials, knowing that he will turn them into triumphs with his redeeming love and faithfulness.

To my family: thank you for your enduring love. You have stood by me always. I pray that all of you will understand now why I felt so strongly about writing this book.

To Larry, my cousin and family minister: you always bring great comfort with your deep, tender voice and loving heart.

Someone's Son
A mother's fight for her gay, drug addicted son

To my dearest friends, Diann and Linda: thank you for your unending love, prayers, and encouragement through it *all*.

To Bret: thank you for being the best friend my son ever had. You are a blessing.

To my friends at Lake Pointe Church, especially the ones in the Stephen Ministry, Marchetti/Steed, and Anderson Life Groups: thank you.

Thanks also to the Ballard and Farmer Life Groups at Chase Oaks Fellowship Church.

To the wonderful people at WinePress Publishing: thank you for your patience with a rookie like me.

To the many special friends and neighbors who have cared and prayed for me and my son on our walk through this fire. I won't try to name you all, I fear that I would leave someone out. You know who you are, and more importantly, God knows who you are. May he bless you richly and eternally.

Most of all, I thank my heavenly Father, who is still teaching me to "rejoice always."

Chapter 1

The Phone Call

The message on my answering machine on Sunday, December 4, 2005, obliterated my already shaky world. "Mom, I'm sick," the voice said. "Can you come and get me? I can't even get a drink of water. Call me."

What now? Ronal Paul, my thirty-four-year-old son, had hit rock bottom so many times I had lost count. His life had become one mess after another—a crystal-meth drug addiction, which led to all sorts of risky behaviors, and now AIDS—messes I had continued to clean up. But I had grown weary of his pleas. I called my close friend, Linda, who had also left a message. "I know it sounds awful," I told her, "but I don't want to call him back." Having walked through this eight-year journey with me, she understood.

In that moment of desperate fatigue over my son's prodigal journey, I had no idea that twenty-four days later Ronal Paul, my only son, would be dead in a Dallas hospital.

But God knew. With my son's weak voice echoing in my ears, I asked God to clarify whether Ronal Paul was crying wolf or if he really needed me. Within minutes, I knew I had to call him back.

His voice rasped when he answered the phone. "I'm . . . having . . . trouble . . . breathing," he said. He barely got out that he had a fever, and then he asked me to come and get him.

I steadied my voice. "Of course I'll come get you." My mind wandered back to the many times Ronal Paul had become belligerent with me and hurled bitter words my way. He would not be an ideal patient. My memory bore the brunt of some of his verbal rages, but it was my heart that bled the most. I pulled in a breath, wondering how it felt to siphon air. Not breathing well was a bad sign. "Let's try to get some medical advice, okay?"

Labored breathing.

Panic.

"Maybe we should go to the hospital," I said.

"I can't go to the . . . emergency . . . room . . . Mom. Can't . . . sit . . . there . . . for hours."

It had been a year since his last visit with an HIV doctor. I was well aware of his distaste for anything having to do with doctors, needles, questions, and procedures, but he had told me he had been meaning to see a doctor about some experimental therapies. I asked him for that doctor's name. He wheezed out that he couldn't remember it, but that he thought he practiced on a particular street. I hung up the phone, and as I did, I prayed that someone would be able to fix his breathlessness.

How had we gotten to this point?

Chapter 2

Growing Up

I lived in Houston, Texas, until 1960, when our family moved to Dallas. Mother, Daddy, my big brother Ronnie, and I embarked on an adventure, leaving everything behind so that Daddy could open a bowling equipment store and thus begin our family business. As Daddy drove up Loop 12 into Casa Linda Shopping Center, my eleven-year-old sensibilities told me that all of Dallas would look like that: stucco and red-tiled roofs. The small profit we had made on our Houston house was seed money for what would eventually become Bowling & Billiard Supplies of Dallas, Inc. That meant several years of living in a rental house.

One evening, Daddy swooped into our home with a smile as broad as Texas. "I did it," he said. "I sold my first bowling ball!" I sat on Mother and Daddy's big bed as my animated father told the story in a way that only he could. Then, in typical Rhodes family fashion, we celebrated with meat loaf, mashed potatoes, and green beans.

Before we moved to Dallas, Mother took us to church because she felt it was her duty. Sometimes Daddy would go with us. One Sunday morning at Spring Branch Baptist Church, I heard Jesus knocking on the door of my heart as our pastor preached. At eight years old, I knew I needed to go forward and accept Jesus as my Savior. As soon as I did, I felt such joy. The congregation witnessed my walk down the aisle to the church's altar, and afterwards folks shook my hand and hugged me.

But in our home we did not live for Christ daily; we simply attended church on Sundays. No one followed up with me, and no one mentored me to grow in my faith. By the time we moved to Dallas, we hardly attended church at all. As a teenager, I tried all the things the other kids did, forgetting my church ways. I don't think I even knew that a personal relationship with Jesus was possible. I didn't know the difference between religion and relationship.

As a boy, Daddy worked the cotton fields—a sticky, hot, laborious task that shaped him in ways I never understood. The work he did as a man, on the other hand, was about as opposite to picking cotton as it could be. Indoors. Air conditioned. No sweaty labor. Add to that my father's zealous love of bowling, and he had found his perfect job. He often said he loved bowling because, unlike most other sports and working in the cotton fields, you did it indoors, and the bowling ball came back to you. Daddy didn't "cotton" much to anything outdoors. Selling his first bowling ball was the icing on his cake.

Daddy worked hard to grow his business, which started as a bowling pro shop. After Daddy bought a barn full of old pool tables, he added billiards, but his personal love was bowling. He lived and breathed and celebrated bowling.

When Ronnie finished high school, Daddy told him, "I don't see any sense in both of us starving. You probably should go find a career." So Ronnie did. He landed several jobs, including one in which he worked on and deciphered new-fangled computers. At one point, he worked for Ross Perot, the founder of Electronic Data Systems. Eventually Bowling & Billiards brought in enough revenue for Daddy to ask Ronnie to join him in the family business.

My life whirled into new possibilities the year we moved to Dallas. I met Diann, my best friend to this day, at Casa View Elementary. A new sense of adventure began seeping into our home, and in it I nursed a secret—a desperate hope that Mother would be happy. Finally.

Today, my mother would probably be diagnosed as bipolar, with a hefty dose of depression and paranoia. Her own mother, my Grandma Nichols, had been an unloving, mean-spirited woman, who often told her that she was never wanted. Mother loved her father, but he was seldom around. She grew up with money but lived in a very unhappy family.

When I think of my mother, I am reminded of that nursery rhyme:

> There was a little girl,
> Who had a little curl,
> Right in the middle of her forehead.
> When she was good,
> She was very good indeed,
> But when she was bad she was horrid.[1]

Mother was a very pretty lady—petite (a trait I did not inherit), quick-witted, and funny. But I don't think she liked herself, so she had trouble liking others in a healthy manner. She had flashes of pure brilliance sometimes, during which her shining face instigated fun and laughter, but her unpredictability set us all on edge. She could be the life of the party or ruin a party in a moment. She took great pride in her appearance but got mad when people told her she looked good. "Well, I certainly don't

---

[1] Henry Wadsworth Longfellow

feel good," she would say. "I wish I felt half as good as people say I look."

Mother had a need to tell everyone her problems, down to the very last detail. Health issues came first, and then came the things that involved me, Ronnie, or Daddy. In her eyes, we could never do right. She had so much to be thankful for but could not seem to appreciate her life. Sad.

Daddy was tall, light, and handsome. He had a winning personality. A born salesman. People of all ages were attracted to him. He loved life and all it held. Most people knew him as Dusty Rhodes. "Dusty" is a common nickname for men with the last name of Rhodes. His legal name was Lorenzo Dow Rhodes. Mother called him "L.D."

Even though my parents never divorced, they came close more than once. I don't know which came first—Mother's emotional problems or Daddy's weakness for women. Mother was emotionally damaged, but was that why Daddy wandered? I'm not sure. She experienced several nervous breakdowns, attempted suicide numerous times, received shock treatments twice, and took many medications to calm her nerves and help her sleep. Often, she would abuse her prescriptions, and every so often Daddy would have to check her into rehab.

At times, Mother would fake being out of her head and act as though she was unable to walk, talk, eat, or communicate. I know this because I would hide outside her bedroom door and watch her primp in front of her mirror, acting perfectly normal until she heard someone coming. Her disassociation from the world and our family would continue for a day, or even several, until she chose to come out of it. In retrospect, I understand that she had been striving to get attention in unhealthy and destructive ways.

Mother didn't love me enough to want to stay on this earth. At least, that was how I felt when I was younger. If she had, why would she have attempted suicide so many times? One of those times continues to haunt me.

Ronnie married and left the house when I was thirteen, so he was no longer around on a daily basis. Just before Thanksgiving of my fifteenth year, Mother and Daddy separated. He fell for another woman and left to pursue her. The night he told us he was leaving was the only time I ever got really mad at him. Ronnie and his wife, Linda, were there also. Mother took to her bed, so we sat around her while Daddy told us his plans.

I raised my voice. "How could you do this to us?" I said. "How do you expect me to take care of Mother? Look at her." I pointed to Mother, who was half alert and half oblivious on the bed.

He softly cried but said very little.

I don't remember saying much else, but I do remember the hurt and disappointment I felt. I knew Mother was difficult, but until then Daddy had never actually left. My daddy, the man I loved more than anything, chose to abandon me. I was left to face Mother's issues alone.

One night, shortly after he left, Mother stuffed towels under our bathroom door. Turning on the gas wall heater, then blocking the entrance, she fell asleep in front of the door. I discovered the closed door in the morning, but when I tried to open it, I could not. I yelled her name but received no response.

With panic stirring in my stomach, I got down on the floor, placed my feet on the door for leverage, and pushed as hard as I could. I cracked open the door just wide enough to reach in and move around her to squeeze through the doorway.

Inside, I found her lying unconscious with a sickly brown discharge coming from her mouth. I bent low, saw the rise and fall of her chest, and thanked God. I pulled her out of the bathroom and into her bedroom, but when I realized that I would not be able to lift her up onto her bed, I called Mrs. Taylor, our neighbor lady, to come and help me.

Mrs. Taylor listened patiently as I explained how I had found her. As we lifted her up onto the bed, her slight frame seemed unusually heavy.

"Should I call an ambulance?" I asked.

"Oh no, Honey. If you do that, it'll be all over the six o'clock news. You don't want that, do you?"

I hadn't thought about that, but even so, I still worried for Mother.

"Why don't we open the window and give her some fresh air," Mrs. Taylor said.

It was the week of Thanksgiving, and it was cold, rainy, and dreary outside. But even as my mom shivered under the open window, I trusted Mrs. Taylor and believed she had the solution to making Mother better.

Mrs. Taylor scooted out almost immediately after reassuring me. "I'm sure she will be all right," she said.

With panic punctuating my words, I called Daddy. He didn't seem bothered or worried. He sighed. "I'll come after work."

I sat in Mother's room all day, watching her snore by the open window, with brown discharge still coming out of her mouth.

When Daddy finally came, he picked her up, laid her in the back seat of the car, and took her to the hospital.

The doctor shook his head when he entered Mother's room. Daddy stood motionless.

"She has a very serious case of pneumonia," the doctor said. "She may not live through the night."

I felt the doctor's words in my chest, and since I had left her under that open window all day, I knew I was to blame.

Daddy took me to my best friend Diann's house to spend the night, but I couldn't sleep because anything that sounded like a ringing phone startled me. I was sure someone was about to call and tell me that Mother was dead.

But she lived.

I never slept well after that because of the constant pressure I felt to wake up and check on her. Sometimes I would find her with her head in the furnace, trying to gas herself again. So I started waiting until after she went to sleep to sneak into her bed and sleep with her. That way, I would know when she got up.

I don't remember anything about Christmas that year, but Daddy came home in January—on my sixteenth birthday. He held Mother and me close and said, "I will never leave you again." And he didn't.

Calvin, my first love, entered my life about a year before Mother tried to kill herself in the bathroom. I spent that terrible Thanksgiving Day with him and his relatives. Calvin was thirteen years old when I met him, and he was already six feet tall. He grew to a slender six-foot-two, with jet-black hair and beautiful blue eyes with dark lashes. In my teenage eyes, he looked like Elvis. I thought he was perfect, except for his tendency to talk too much. That boy couldn't keep a secret. He even spilled the beans about my surprise Sweet Sixteen party.

One time, we went with Daddy to make a delivery to a local bowling center. We watched people bowl while Daddy talked to the guy at the desk. I turned around to say something to Calvin, but when I did, I realized he hadn't been watching people bowl as I had. Instead, he had been leaning against the counter, looking at me with the most intense look of love I had ever seen. It was a look I would never forget.

We were madly in love with each other, but eventually he shattered my heart. "Maybe we should see other people," he told me one afternoon after I had turned sixteen.

I stormed away furiously, determined to meet someone new that day. And I did. That night, while Diann and I cruised the high spots of suburban East Dallas, we spied a Dairy Queen®, and I met Bobby.

Someone's Son
A mother's fight for her gay, drug addicted son

I drove a 1955 Thunderbird, which attracted a lot of attention. We parked just far enough away from Dairy Queen's® entrance to be seen. Bobby sat in the back seat of a car that circled us a few times and then parked in front of the restaurant. Diann and I both thought the guy in the back seat was cute. The couple in the car's front seat went in to the Dairy Queen®. The cute guy got out and walked toward my car. He knelt down on the passenger side where Diann sat and turned on his charm.

"Would you girls like to talk to a poor, mistreated little boy?" He tried to brush his hair out of his face but poked himself in the eye in the process. "See, I even pick on myself." He laughed.

We all laughed. He told us his name was Robert Britt, but most people called him Bobby. As the conversation continued, he walked, or I should say *strutted*, to my side of the car. He was James Dean personified—a nineteen-year-old bad boy who ignited excitement in me. He was average height, slim, and really cute, with nice brown eyes, a dark complexion, and brown hair. I gave him my phone number.

Although Diann initially thought Bobby was good-looking, it didn't take long for her to form an opinion: she flat out did not have a good feeling about him. Both Ronnie and my parents agreed.

Bobby came from a broken home—his parents had divorced when he was young. His father left one night to go to the grocery store for ice cream and never returned. Bobby had very little memory of his dad, an alcoholic who died homeless on the streets in Chicago many years after the divorce. The city contacted Bobby's mother, Frances, to ask if she wanted to claim his body, but she had neither the money nor the desire to do so. Frances did the best she could raising two children by herself, working split shifts and late nights at Southwestern Bell® as a long-distance operator. The family lived in a rough part of

Dallas, so Bobby and his sister, Gaila, scraped together a street education. Both experienced little supervision or discipline.

The lack of an important foundation led Bobby into brushes with the law as well as several addictions, but I was naïve enough to think I could change him. After nearly two years of putting up with his trouble-making ways, however, I realized I could not. The initial impressions of Diann and my family rang true. I broke up with Bobby for good.

Then . . . I missed a few periods and started to panic. I didn't know where to turn. I certainly could not turn to my mother and be forced to hear her guilt-inducing comments. Nor could I bear to break my daddy's heart.

I didn't know what my brother Ronnie would say, so I gathered the courage to tell my sister-in-law, Linda, who was pregnant with their first child, Eddie.

"I think I might be pregnant," I told her. My heart beat like crazy in my chest. I tried to swallow my fear.

After hugging and crying with me, Linda made arrangements to take me to her doctor the next day to find out for sure.

"Come spend the night with us," she said.

"Please don't tell Ronnie," I begged.

"I have to," she said. "He'll wonder why you're spending the night." So she told him. I told Mother that I was spending the night with Diann and then alerted Diann to cover for me in case she called.

Getting ready for bed that night, I heard Ronnie's footsteps outside the room where I would sleep. He knocked gently and then sat on my bed. "Brenda," he said, "I want you to know that I'll be there, whatever you decide to do."

"Really?" I didn't expect such kindness, since I knew he must have been disappointed in me.

"Whether you keep the baby and not marry Bobby, keep the baby and marry Bobby, or give the baby up for adoption, I'll be there for you."

Adoption? That thought had never entered my mind.

I couldn't respond. I just cried and cried, not knowing what I would do if I found out I was pregnant.

After performing a pelvic exam, the doctor knew. "You *are* pregnant," he told me. I got dressed and entered his office.

"You should put this baby up for adoption. It's the proper thing to do. The right thing."

I bristled at his words. Although the news of my pregnancy rang freshly in my ears, I knew one thing: I would keep my baby. Bobby's baby.

"Doctor," I said, choking on my tears, "I can't do that. I will keep my baby."

Calvin and I had remained friends. That evening, I called him in tears, and he came over quickly. "I'm pregnant," I told him. "With Bobby's child."

We cried together and held each other for a long, long time.

He held me a moment more and said, "Baby, I love you. I will always love you. Marry me, not him."

It was a sweet offer, but I think he knew that I could not or *would* not accept. Only if Bobby rejected me would I have ever considered such a proposal.

But Bobby did not reject me when I told him the news.

And then I told my parents I wanted to marry Bobby and asked them to sign for me. At that time in Texas, a girl had to be eighteen years old to get married without parental permission, and a boy had to be twenty-one.

"After being broken up for a while," I told my parents, "Bobby promised me he would change, and I believe him."

"You believe him?" Mother and Daddy asked disgustedly. They would not give their consent.

"I'll wait," I told them. "I will marry him next month when I'm eighteen."

One night, Daddy and I met in the hallway. He took me by the arm, and with compassion he looked me straight in the eyes. "Is there some reason why this wedding is so urgent?" he asked.

"No, Daddy," I lied. "I want to marry Bobby. We love each other."

My parents must have sensed they couldn't stop me, so they offered to have the wedding at our house. Bobby's mom, Frances, had to sign for Bobby since he was just shy of twenty-one, but she knew about the pregnancy and was fine with the marriage.

We married five days after my eighteenth birthday—on January 20, 1967. Of course, when we told my parents about the pregnancy shortly thereafter, they were not surprised. But at least I did not have to live in the same house with Mother anymore and listen to her rant about how I could have done such a thing to her.

My daughter, Wendi, came hollering into the world five months later—on June 22, 1967. Beautiful. She looked just like her daddy.

Chapter 3

Life with Bobby

Wendi's daddy had his own set of baggage. He still struggled with drugs and various other addictions, and he gave himself over to petty crime.

In light of all that, Bobby's sister, Gaila, invited us to go to church with her at Oak Cliff Assembly of God. She was very concerned about Bobby's direction and knew we needed the Lord in our lives. At the time, she was a serious Christian. After attending church with her several times, both Bobby and I recommitted our lives to Jesus Christ. For the first time, we experienced a loving, close marriage.

I stayed involved with the Charismatic church for several years, and overall it was a good experience. I learned a lot about the Bible, and my faith strengthened. The Rhodes family did not understand or like the church's atmosphere, and Bobby's mother mostly made fun of it. My parents thought I was going overboard, but I did receive a good foundation there and do not regret the experience. The only thing I disliked about that church was that it preached fear over love. It was more about the devil than God. I felt that if I said the word "damn," I might go to hell. For that reason, I did not get a good understanding of God's grace.

But even though I pursued God, Bobby couldn't seem to connect his life to his beliefs. His faith during those six months was real, but he was weak and soon drifted. He went to jail many times for unpaid traffic tickets. One of those times, the police came to pick him up, waited for him to finish showering and dressing, and then took him in. After he left, I realized he had parked his truck behind my car and taken his keys with him. Because I was his Great Enabler, I pushed his truck out into the street against the curb, grabbed Wendi, and bailed him out of jail—all while being two months pregnant with Ronal Paul!

Bobby never held a job for long. He always complained that he didn't like what he was doing or didn't care for his boss. He argued and incited fights. Daddy even hired him, but since Bobby didn't think he should start at the bottom, he didn't last long. Daddy got him jobs at both Mrs. Baird's Bakery and at Sherwin Williams Paint, but Bobby either quit or got fired again and again. I was so embarrassed all the time.

During the time that Bobby was running from job to job, my mother came for a visit—a rare thing for her, but she knew I was pregnant again, and she was worried. She looked in the pantry and fridge, stormed out of the house without saying a word, and returned with a load of groceries.

"How could you be so stupid?" Each unloaded grocery sack became an exclamation point. "How could you marry such a sorry excuse for a man?"

When Bobby came home and discovered the fridge and pantry stocked, he flew into a rage and dialed Mother. "I can take care of my own family," he told her.

But the truth was that he could not—or would not.

I remembered one of the comments Mother made when we told her we wanted to get married: "You want to marry *my*

daughter? Why, you can't even afford to keep her in *panty hose!*"
True words, those.

Someone had to provide for our family, and I had always
been a good worker. From age sixteen to nineteen, I worked as
a long-distance operator at Southwestern Bell®. Then I worked
in accounting at Gaylord Container Corporation for ten years.
I provided for the family during the day and tried to maintain
the home at night, but I wasn't a very good housekeeper. Bobby
refused to help around the house at all. I even mowed the lawn
and took out the trash while he lay on the couch, drinking
beer, smoking pot, and watching TV. What a life.

I never knew when he was going to come home at night, and
he never called to let me know his whereabouts. Many nights
I loaded Wendi into the car and ventured from bar to bar to
look for his pickup truck. If I spied it, I did not go in. Instead,
I returned home, knowing where he was. If I did not find him,
I dialed the jails and hospitals. Eventually I stopped doing
that. Instead, I lay in bed worrying, unable to sleep, wishing
he would disappear like his father. I often fantasized about the
police knocking on the front door at a late hour, with hats in
their hands and downcast eyes, telling me that Bobby had been
killed in an accident.

But he always came home eventually, and I had to deal with
my deeply conflicting emotions. I was mad, relieved, and disappointed all at the same time. One night, as he crawled into
bed next to me, I rolled over and said, "Are you ever going to
grow up and think of others instead of only yourself?"

In the darkness, he replied, "Hell, no."

Bobby did not take naturally to fatherhood. Kids made him
nervous. They cried and had endless needs that he had no capacity to meet. He loved Wendi as much as he was capable of
loving anyone. He would swing her around and throw her up
in the air from time to time. She giggled when he did, and, like
any little girl, she loved her daddy.

Someone's Son
A mother's fight for her gay, drug addicted son

One evening, when I was five months pregnant with Ronal Paul, Bobby and I were watching TV. I had already put Wendi to bed for the night. Bobby looked at me and said, "I don't think I love you anymore. I'm leaving." He stood up, gathered a few of his personal things, and left. Just like that.

I didn't say a word. I just sat there, stunned, for who knows how long.

Wendi missed him terribly. She would stand at the front window, press her tiny hand to the glass, and cry for her daddy. It broke my heart.

A few days before my due date, I went over to Mother and Daddy's house to stay with them. On February 26, 1971, I went into labor. They drove me to the hospital. My brother Ronnie woke me up after delivery with a big, proud smile on his face. "You have a red-headed baby boy," he said.

I think I said something silly, like, "Does he have freckles?" I had always hated my freckles.

I found out later that a nurse mistook Ronnie for the father, since he was the youngest man in the waiting room. She grabbed him by the arm and said, "Come on, Dad. Let's go wake up Mom." Ronnie didn't argue, and I was glad he didn't.

I divorced Bobby shortly after Ronal Paul was born.

Ronal Paul had a sweet nature about him that everyone noticed the moment they saw him. There was something about his countenance that seemed calm and serene. A peaceful child.

Fast forward a few years to 1973. On Ronal Paul's second birthday, Bobby was arrested for armed robbery. He and an accomplice had robbed two Safeway® stores at gunpoint—one in Denton, the other in Sherman.

I did not intend to visit or communicate with him, but Gaila kept after me to go and see him.

"He really wants to see you," she told me.

I shook my head while Ronal Paul chased Wendi through our home.

"I'm serious," she said. "He's hit the bottom this time. I think he'll finally turn around. He needs you."

She persisted for several weeks until she wore me down. I finally agreed to go visit him at the Grayson County Jail in Sherman, Texas. In that jail, you could visit an inmate in a room without being separated by glass barriers. You could even touch each other and be alone—with a guard outside your door, of course. I noticed the plain room, which seemed very cold—just a table and four chairs, one barred window, and no pictures on the walls. To add to the starkness, they had painted the concrete walls white.

I prayed a lot in preparation for our meeting. Alone, I fidgeted with my hands as I waited for him to enter the room. As soon as he walked through the door, my heart melted. He looked so pitiful in his baggy white clothes. I guess I expected black and white stripes. On the back of his shirt, in large black letters, were the words "Grayson County Jail."

He didn't try to approach me.

"Thanks for coming," he said, averting his eyes.

Neither of us sat; we stood the entire visit.

"I'm sorry," he said.

I didn't respond. I prayed quietly.

"For all I've done," Bobby continued. "I let you down. I let the kids down. I haven't been responsible. Haven't been the man God wants me to be."

His words were barely above a whisper, but I felt them in my soul, took them in, and wanted to believe every single sentence.

He lifted his eyes—those James Dean rebel eyes that now looked sheepish and needy—and I asked myself what kind of woman would turn away such a repentant man.

"Give me another chance," he said.

Still, I faltered. "I just don't know, Bobby."

Tears formed in his eyes. "I'll prove it. I promise. I'm okay with God now. And he wants us to be a real family."

Oh, how I wanted that! As a single mom raising two children, I wanted a family. It was all I ever wanted, the thing I valued most—a responsible husband, two loving kids, and a home that was intact.

Bobby and I talked our allowed hour. I didn't commit right then. The stark room did not hear me beg or plead; it only heard the sound of my own silence. But I did leave him with this: "Bobby?"

"Yes?" His downcast eyes melted my resolve.

"I'll consider what you've said. I promise."

He approached me and held me tightly. I felt his heartbeat against mine, all the while begging God to make this all come out right. Wasn't God in the habit of making all things new? Was this his direction? His plan? I wondered if Bobby was genuine. If he had hit bottom, had he truly changed and come back to God? In his embrace, all my questions melted.

I was falling again.

I visited Bobby in that white room every week. Before long, he asked me to remarry him. I agreed. Since he had become friends with the sheriff, Bobby was made a trustee and given more freedom. His turnaround seemed complete. Bobby and I could go into the jail's kitchen, pop popcorn, and then take it to his private cell to eat, talk, and plan our new life together. I felt deep happiness, even though my parents and Ronnie thought I was crazy. They worried about my future—and for good reason.

My pastor visited Bobby on a regular basis. He also drove up from Dallas to marry us. The sheriff arranged for us to be married in a local church, he even allowed Bobby to wear street clothes for the ceremony. On May 11, 1973, the sheriff drove us to the church, and our pastor married us. My brokenhearted parents, our two kids, and Bobby's mother, Frances, witnessed.

How beautiful! What a testimony to God's ability to turn a
life around. I wore a short, baby-blue dress and a long "fall"—
a partial wig—since Bobby liked my hair straight, not curly.
I looked like a country-western singer marrying a country
bumpkin.

As I write this, I find myself shaking my head. Don't you just
hate looking back on the stupid things you did when you were
young? I know I do.

Bobby was sent to Huntsville, a Texas state penitentiary. In
the five years he lived there, I missed only one visiting day,
and that was only because Wendi had bladder surgery. We
anxiously waited for him to come home so we could finally be
a real family. I built up his return to the kids, telling them that
things would be great when Daddy came home. I expected it.
I hoped for it. I knew everything would be picture perfect. But
it only took a few months of freedom for Bobby to rediscover
his affection for drugs.

The kids didn't know he was using, but he suddenly lost all
interest in them and our daily life. As part of Bobby's parole,
Ronnie had provided him with a job, but it didn't last. Then a
friend found him a job with a freight-lines company. It worked
out until they fired him for selling pot to other employees.

Within months, I was reliving the same-old, sad story of an
addict husband who couldn't hold down a job.

One day, I hefted in a heavy load of groceries from the car
while Bobby reclined on the couch—his throne of late. He
didn't stir and didn't offer to help. I rushed to the kitchen, seeth-
ing with anger, hoping not to drop anything. But I dropped a
bag. A jar of pickles shattered on the kitchen floor, splashing
pickles and juice everywhere.

Bobby lifted his head, looked at me, and said, "You stupid
broad."

That was the breaking point. Out he went, that day!

I have a habit of taking too much, but when I'm done, I'm done.

When the divorce finalized, the judge ordered him to pay eighty dollars a month in child support.

"But judge," Bobby said, "I can't pay that. I don't have a job."

"Then you'd better find one," the judge ordered.

He never paid child support.

Chapter 4

Ronal Paul, the Tenderhearted Outcast

During Bobby's incarceration, his mother, Frances, lived with us. Although she and Bobby's sister, Gaila, adored Wendi (who was the spitting image of her daddy), they did not take to Ronal Paul, who was more like a Rhodes—fair complexion, red hair, and an easy-going disposition.

When I first got pregnant with Ronal Paul, Bobby and I decided that if the baby were a boy we would name him Robert Paul and call him Little Bob. This was during the time that we were both walking with God, and I had sincere hope for the future. After Bobby left Wendi and me, however, I couldn't bear the thought of naming the baby after his father.

Knowing it would be an uncomfortable conversation, I did not tell that to Frances. When Ronal Paul was born, I named him after my brother Ronnie, with a slight difference in spelling. This angered Frances. She never liked Ronnie much, and one of Bobby's wayward childhood friends shared the same name. She blamed the naming decision on my mother, which only fueled the animosity between the Britt and Rhodes families.

Someone's Son
A mother's fight for her gay, drug addicted son

I wanted to call my son Ron Paul, but Frances never would. She called him Paul. Being the peacemaker—or better put, the doormat—I let it be. The Britt family called him Paul, and that was the name he went by in school. The Rhodes family called him Ronal Paul.

Both Gaila and Frances doted on Wendi but merely tolerated Ronal Paul. The kids spent a lot of time at Gaila's house during the summers, since I had to work. Ronal Paul became an outcast there. Looking back, it seemed like Wendi belonged to them and Ronal Paul belonged to me.

They made it obvious that Wendi mattered more to them than Ronal Paul. One day while Frances lived with us, she brought home a whole bag of clothes and toys for Wendi. Wendi jumped up and down, picking through the packages and squealing with delight over each new thing. Over to the side, Ronal Paul waited patiently for his package, but none came. When I realized this, I reached out and hugged him. "Mommy will take you shopping for your own treasures. How would you like that?"

He nodded.

I looked up at Frances, shooting her an angry-mother look. She just shrugged her shoulders and walked into her room.

Gaila permitted her kids and Wendi to do anything they wanted, but she ruthlessly corrected Ronal Paul. Her sons would hit him, and he had to take it. If he hit back, she got furious.

"You can't treat him that way," I told her. "You can't just correct him and let everyone else get away with everything. It's not fair. He doesn't deserve that."

"I don't know what you're talking about," she replied. "I've never done that!" Many years later, she apologized to him and to me for her mistreatment.

I tried to make it up to him with my love, but I smothered him, protecting him from their obvious and painful favoritism.

Ronal Paul, the Tenderhearted Outcast

I have often said that my biggest mistake with Ronal Paul became loving him too much. He was my joy, my confidante my rock. He was such a sweet, easygoing little guy, always making the best of every situation. And he loved everything and everyone.

He had an artistic, inquisitive nature. He'd spy an unusual flower or a leaf and show it to me. We had a schefflera plant in the house by our front door. Whenever it sprouted a new little baby leaf, Ronal Paul and I would make a big fuss over how cute it was. Wendi would tell us how silly we were, but we didn't care. It became a funny event between the three of us each time we spotted a new leaf.

Since circumstances kept him surrounded by women, his friends during his growing-up years were almost exclusively girls. This progressed to high school, where girls seemed to follow him around. Wendi used to say he'd make a great husband, considering his sensitivity and artistic bent, his tender heart.

But throughout all this, he didn't take to boy things. When the other boys in the family enjoyed hunting and sports, it just didn't seem to be his thing. Protecting was. Once, after staying up really late watching infomercials as a teen, he took my credit card and made a payment to help orphans. He told me the next morning what he had done, with tears in his eyes, still sad for the fly-infested hungry orphans. That's the kind of tenderhearted kid he was.

In addition to singlehandedly solving the world's orphan problem using my credit card, he also took to fixing broken creatures. When he was seven, I gave him and Wendi two baby ducks for Easter. We housed them in a cage that I hefted onto the air-conditioning unit outside so our dachshund, Pebbles, couldn't terrorize, torment, or even kill them. One day Ronal Paul checked on the ducks, only to return hollering and crying.

"Mom, Pebbles snatched one of our ducks and chewed up its bill!"

I assessed the poor duckling's situation. The bottom part of its bill hung loosely, fully mangled. His tiny tongue, meant to be housed in the safe confines of its bill, dangled free. I knelt on the grass that had recently changed from Texas winter-brown to springtime green, wondering how to tell my inconsolable son the duck's inevitable fate. "Son, I'm sorry, but this duck is probably going to die. It can't eat. It can't drink. Not with its bill like this."

But he would have none of my careful words.

"I'll fix him," he said.

He bound the bill with bandages, only to have the duck finagle his way out. He taped the bill, but the duck Houdinied his way free. He crafted splints from Popsicle® sticks, but the duck refused his efforts.

Finally, he realized he could do nothing to repair the duck, so he took to educating the poor fowl. He tried to train the duck to eat and drink with its tongue hanging loose, but the duck simply couldn't follow Ronal Paul's instructions. He worked all afternoon, coaxing, pleading, helping, only to watch the duck defy his efforts and die in spite of his persistent love.

Today, I wish I didn't know how that feels.

Chapter 5

When I Couldn't Fix
Daddy

Anyone who knows me will tell you this: I am, or was, a Daddy's girl. My world pivoted around this man who laughed easily, worked hard, and could light up a room when he entered it. I take it as the best compliment when folks say I'm like him. And the best compliment I can give a person is that he reminds me of my father.

Daddy was tall, handsome, and smart. He was a big man—not just in stature, but in heart. He not only learned his smarts from school but also from sheer determination. He burst with integrity and character and had the most brilliant business mind of anyone I've ever known. He could remember anyone's name. He'd remember meeting you three years ago, then address you by name and ask specific questions about your life. That was Daddy—everyone's friend.

As a little girl, I thrilled when he lifted me on his shoulders. Not because I could see the world from a bird's eye view, but because I felt Daddy's strength and his love while I sat up there. His lap became the perfect place to curl up on, and he would bounce me on his knees until I laughed. He danced with me, my small feet on his. That man, oh how I loved him, and he loved me!

Even at twenty-seven years old, Daddy called me his little girl. He loved me unconditionally. I know he wasn't perfect, but his love for me never wavered. As I mentioned earlier, Daddy had a weakness for the ladies, drawn to his good looks and personality, and in that he faltered more than once.

Daddy's cancer went undiagnosed by Dallas-area doctors for a long time. They told him that his symptoms of dizziness and dragging one leg came from stress. He started having problems six-to-eight months before going to Houston to find the right doctor. One Sunday in the summer of 1976, the kids and I dined at Red Lobster with Mother and Daddy. He told us, "I know there is something wrong with me."

I wanted to tell him stress made him sick, but something inside me knew his intuition was correct.

"I heard there's a doctor in Houston really good at diagnosing people when no one else can," he said. "I want to go see him."

He made an appointment to go to the clinic in Houston the same week I had planned a vacation with the kids at Lake Murray Lodge in Oklahoma, something we looked forward to, since it would be our first real vacation. But I had a strong feeling I should go with Mother and Daddy. I canceled the vacation. I hated to disappoint the kids, but I knew I had to go to Houston, especially since Ronnie and Linda would be at a bowling convention in New Orleans.

The new doctor in Houston examined Daddy by running a series of external tests: watching him walk, having him follow his finger with his eyes without moving his head, and giving him a simple memory and math test. Daddy had an excellent memory and was a whiz with numbers, but he did not do well on these tests and did not realize that he performed poorly. I watched closely.

After the short exam, the doctor said abruptly, "Mr. Rhodes, I believe you have a brain tumor. If I am right, and if it is operable, do you want me to fix it?" Mother and I thought it was a strange question, and so did Daddy.

He looked at the doctor in a puzzled way and answered, "That's why I'm here."

The doctor explained that they would run some tests tomorrow, and then they'd know more about what we faced and how to deal with it. Then he walked out of the room.

Mother and I visited with Daddy a little longer. I tried to be positive about the situation. Mother said very little. And for the first time in my life, Daddy looked scared. My big, brave father was frightened. I had never seen that look in his eyes before, and it would not be the last time. Mother and I returned to our motel room for the night. Oddly, I was concerned, but not terribly scared. If he had a brain tumor, at least we knew the problem and could get it fixed. Right?

Daddy would be fine. I was sure of that. We didn't even call Ronnie, opting to wait for the tests the next day. Mother called "Aunt" Susie, her best friend who lived in Houston, so she could fill her in on what the doctor told us.

During one of the tests the next day, Daddy had a convulsion. A serious convulsion that crushed several vertebrae in his back. They stopped the test and rushed him to ICU.

"We found two brain tumors," the doctor said in the aftermath of Daddy's seizure. "And we suspect the source of the tumor is in his lungs."

Hearing that stopped my heart. His brain *and* his lungs?

"I'll have to be honest with you. His prognosis is not good."

I pulled in a breath, tried to steady myself. Mother didn't speak. So I asked, "What do you mean?

"Most people with this diagnosis don't live more than six months."

"What?" The hallway around me started closing in. My head buzzed.

Then the doctor stated, "He is younger and stronger than most in this condition, so maybe he will live longer. But this is terminal."

Terminal? That word could not be associated with *my* daddy. No, I could not believe what I was hearing.

"Should I call my brother?" I steadied myself by touching the hospital's sterile hallway.

"He is not in danger of going right now, so that is up to you." The doctor and his team rushed off down the hall. They dropped a bomb on us then just walked away.

Aunt Susie heard the news alongside us. We walked into the waiting room and sat down.

I called Ronnie. Linda answered. "Hi. Can I talk to Ronnie?" I tried to steady my voice, to be strong.

He came to the phone and with a very positive, uplifting voice said, "Good Morning!" It was afternoon, but my brother answers that way when he is in a good mood.

I held myself together enough to tell him what the doctors had just told us. His response? Silence. Complete silence.

"Ronnie, are you there?"

He cleared his throat. "Do they know that he is not your normal guy on the street? Do they know they are dealing with an exceptional man? I'll be there as soon as I can get there." He hung up.

I looked at Mother and Aunt Susie. "I need to go to the car to get some things." Aunt Susie, bless her heart, came with me. As we walked outside, the world seemed unreal. Car noises echoed in the distance. I heard a loud, constant, deep humming in my head. I existed on autopilot—a machine without emotion. We walked in silence through the underground parking garage, to the car. It was hot, humid.

I opened the car's rear door, collapsed on the seat, and cried uncontrollably. Aunt Susie placed her hand on my back, trying to comfort me while I coughed and gagged and wept harder than I thought possible. I'm sure my sobs echoed throughout the parking garage. I didn't know if I would ever stop.

When I finally gained control of myself, I was so glad that Aunt Susie left Mother in the waiting room and followed to comfort me. She seemed to know just what to do, allowing me to get everything out. She'd known I would need her more than Mother would, so she came with me.

I never saw Mother break down. I hate to say it, but the world still pivoted around her, as if she were oblivious to her husband's condition and prognosis. When we visited his room, she would tell him what a hard night *she* had, how she couldn't sleep, didn't feel good, how tired she was and so on. I couldn't believe it.

But still, Daddy often told me, "Don't let your mother overdo it. Take care of her."

Ronnie was determined that Daddy would win this battle. He made sure, to the best of his ability, that the medical community did everything possible. Every intervention, drug, therapy, conferences with other doctors, anything that might result in a different prognosis. He stayed with him more than I did after that first week because I had to get back to work, but since he worked for the family business, he had some flexibility. Ronnie made Daddy feed himself and shave himself, determined to help him get stronger.

I visited every weekend. Of course, I was coming to Huntsville to visit Bobby every other weekend, anyway—at the time of Daddy's hospitalization we were still married.

One time when Daddy and I walked down the hall to a waiting room he asked me, "What do the doctors say my chances are?"

None of us told him the doctor's prognosis. Ronnie didn't want us to give him any bad news yet. We only answered his direct questions. He hadn't ask this particular question yet, at least not to me. I took a deep breath and said,

"They are going to do all they can, Daddy."

He looked straight ahead and said, "I see."

He went back and forth from Dallas to Houston for those last few months. But Daddy was in the Houston hospital when he learned his mother, Grandma Rhodes, died. He was too sick to go to his own mother's funeral. He had always been the leader in the family, the one to make the decisions. Everyone leaned on him and depended on him, and now he could do nothing to help. He called me at work and cried on the phone. "I didn't even get a chance to see her, and now she's gone," he said.

I tried to comfort him the best I could. But all the while, crying inside, I knew my big, strong daddy was slipping away.

I couldn't bear to see my father so sick. Until his cancer, he lived life strong and happy-go-lucky, brimming with life and energy. And how he loved his grandchildren! He always said he had a blond, a brunette, a red-head, and a cotton-top—Eddie, Wendi, Ronal Paul and Shelley. My kids and I spent many weekends at Mother and Daddy's house. They really loved their Papaw because he acted like a great big kid with them. He and Ronal Paul were buddies, I loved watching Daddy with the kids because he was a very loving grandfather. His only problem? His soft heart. He'd let them get away with anything, all while Mother fussed at him. Which just made all three want to get into more mischief.

If anyone could overcome illness with a positive attitude, Daddy could. The doctors told us that he would lose his mental faculties, but they didn't know my father. His mind stayed sharp during the entire ordeal. He knew each one of us and called all the nurses by name.

One weekend the doctor told me they were going to do a lung biopsy. "But he's so weak, he may not survive," he said.

"Why is it necessary then? You need to talk to my brother on Monday before you do anything." I went back to the room to see Daddy.

That was the last day I spent with him. We were alone. He talked as much as he could, and I attended to him as he needed. He said again, "Take care of your mother." I shuddered as I gave him my word, though I worried if I had the wherewithal to honor his request.

Every so often, I slipped into the bathroom to cry, though I held in my voice so he couldn't hear me.

I tried to freshen my face before I went back into his room. I took a deep breath. Each time I looked at him, my heart nearly burst with grief. "Is there anything else you want me to do for you, Daddy?"

"Yes," he said. "Just sit here on the bed and let me look at you."

"Okay," I replied, as perky as I could.

So I sat there and held his hand and smiled at him until he drifted off to sleep. Then I returned to the bathroom, spilling more tears. When he woke up, it was time for me to go. I said, "Bye, Daddy. I'll see you later."

"I know you will, Sugar."

We both knew what we meant. When I left that day, we knew it was probably the last time we would see each other on this earth.

As I drove the long journey back to Dallas, I cried most of the way and begged God not to take him. I said, "But I trust You, and I'll accept whatever Your will is." The words echoed off my car windows, and I knew right then I had lied to God. I didn't want his will. I wanted Daddy. Alive.

The following Wednesday, ten days after Grandma Rhodes died, I sat at my desk at work and looked up. Linda stood in the doorway of the office. I knew immediately Daddy had died. Linda had never been to my work, and her presence could only mean bad news.

I didn't want to hear what she had to say. I got up quickly. We walked back out into the lobby and hugged and softly cried. Instantly, I felt my heart harden. How could God do this? *Why* would God do this? Daddy was only fifty-nine years old.

Funny how you can recount the very moment you backed away from God. For me it was September 29, 1976. When Daddy left the earth, he took my heart with him—and my desire to follow my heavenly Father. How could God do this? Daddy loved life more than anyone I'd ever known. We all loved him and needed him. My kids needed their grandfather, especially Ronal Paul. He never stopped missing his Papaw. His death wasn't fair.

For twenty-three years, starting from the day Linda told me Daddy died, I consciously rebelled. I made a choice to live my life as I chose. I even began to doubt God's existence. It didn't matter. I didn't need him anyway. I was just fine by myself. Daddy-less, but fine.

Chapter 6

Mother's Suicide
Attempt—Again

After Daddy's death, the business went through difficulties. He'd been its driving force, so in his absence the buzzards circled. The banks were scared. Mother worried—a lot. Even Ronnie was deeply concerned. For the next three years, the business dove up and down, but we endured, even when bankruptcy threatened.

Ronnie stepped in to lead the company in Daddy's absence and did a phenomenal job. In 1978 I went to work with Ronnie. We became close and worked together very well. Under his tutelage, the business grew and experienced success.

Mother lived alone after Daddy's death, experiencing fears about the business. She had difficulty coping with the stress, even with Ronnie at the helm. She didn't trust anyone. Her emotional problems grew, burying her under grief and worry.

The Garland Police Department called me one Sunday morning, two years after Daddy's death. "Your mother has attempted suicide with a straight razor," the officer said. "She called and told us what she had done. She asked us to call you, then I believe she passed out."

I couldn't understand his words, how they ran together. Razor. Passed out. Call me. Mother didn't even own a straight razor, or so I thought. I pulled in a few frightened breaths, then I found my voice. "Where is she now?"

"The ambulance took her to Baylor Hospital," he said.

"Thanks, I'd better go."

"Wait," he said. "You really ought to come to the house first and clean up the blood before it starts to stink. It'll be harder to clean up after it's dried."

I think I said something like "thanks for the advice" and hung up, then drove straight to Baylor.

Ronnie was deer hunting in a remote area. I couldn't reach him by phone, so I left a message with someone to have him call me. Mother was still in the emergency room when I arrived. Her feet were caked in dried blood. Her glasses, still on her face, were splattered red. The EMTs had bandaged her arms where she'd made the cuts. They placed her blood-soaked nightgown in a plastic bag by her gurney.

Sometime during the day, Ronnie called.

"Mother tried to kill herself again, Ronnie." I tried to describe what had happened but had a hard time finding the words. "She was covered in blood. Where did she get a straight razor?"

"Brenda, listen to me. Do *not* go into the house by yourself."

"Why?"

"Just don't do it. I'll call Elva."

Elva was our dear cleaning lady we employed at Bowling & Billiards. She also cleaned Mother's house, so she had a key. Ronnie made me promise not to go to the house.

But as I drove home from Baylor, I wondered about Elva. I wanted to see how the cleaning had progressed, so I drove to Mother's. Elva's car wasn't in the driveway. Still, I went in.

I wish I hadn't.

Mother's home looked like the scene of a hatchet massacre, blood everywhere—on the walls, the carpet—almost over the entire house. Upon further throat-choking inspection, I realized she had sat in the bathtub in the hallway bathroom, held each arm on the side of the tub, and cut herself several times. Blood ran down the tub on both sides. She must've gotten scared and left the bloody bathtub to call for help. Bloody hand prints smeared their way down the long hall.

She had ventured into the bathroom in her bedroom and stood at the sink, bleeding into it and all over the floor. Then she must've crossed the bedroom to get to the phone by her bed. She sat on the bed and bled another pool on the floor. After calling for help, she sprawled across the bed and bled through the sheets and the mattress pad, onto the mattress.

So much blood, I thought. How could one person lose that much blood and still live? The violence of the act made me sick, physically and emotionally.

When Elva got there, she immediately asked me to leave. She pulled the mattress out into the back yard, turned the water hose on it, and started scrubbing.

But nothing could scrub away the memory of my mother's blood from my mind. Soon after, I brought Mother to live with us, so I could make sure this didn't happen again.

Chapter 7

More Marriages and More about Mother

In 1980 I met Con. We will call him that for the purposes of this book. You will learn why later. After dating three months, we married on the 4th of July in Las Vegas. He swept me off my feet with his romantic and fun-loving personality.

I felt happier than I had ever been. On our first Valentine's Day, Con—with the enlisted help of Ronal Paul—crafted a giant, red-crepe paper heart on the roof of our house. Even more sentimental than I was, he wrote me poems, saved photos, movie receipts, and restaurant souvenirs from everywhere we went. Each year on our anniversary, he created a large card from these collections, cutting out words and pictures from magazines, and gluing everything just so.

In addition to these thoughtful traits, he owned his own business. He was the anti-Bobby. He made everything an adventure, even grocery shopping or standing in long lines. As a magician, he'd entertain everyone with his sleight-of-hand magic.

One Christmas, he gave me a parachute jump. And, yes, later that spring I did jump out of a perfectly good airplane. He scratched my back every night if I wanted, which I loved. He even cut my toenails! He was a very capable, take-charge man. I wanted someone to help me in my personal life, to relieve me of some of my responsibilities. In every way, he treasured me, making sure I felt safe, secure, and cared for.

He clashed with Wendi, but I dismissed it. After all, she was entering her teen years. He and Ronal Paul got along fine. Or so I thought.

But issues erupted when we moved to a new home in 1982. During that transaction, I learned Con had bad credit. He had a way of explaining it away that made sense to me, so I dismissed it.

Until the barrage of phone calls interrupted our new home.

Creditors could now find him, since the mortgage listed his name and contact information. All hours of the day and night, they called, bullied, and harassed. In my family and family business we prided ourselves on good fiscal integrity. What made this more humiliating: In my position over accounts receivable at Bowling & Billiards, I had to deal every day with people who dodged their responsibilities. Now I was married to one of them!

Then Con's women issues began. Wendi told me that he had solicited one of her friend's mothers to go out of town with him.

"Con, what's going on?" I asked him the next morning after Wendi's revelation.

Sitting across from me at the breakfast table, he averted his eyes. "What do you mean?"

"Wendi tells me you asked her friend's mom to leave town with you."

He fidgeted a bit then looked me square in the face, unflinching. "Oh, Brenda, you know how I am. She took me seriously? I was just teasing, is all. I didn't mean it!" He roared his laughter in such a way that I believed him. Of course he wouldn't solicit another woman. There must have been a misunderstanding. But still, I wondered.

Not long after, Ronnie pulled me into his office. He sat, his face serious, his fingers tented, his jaw clenching. He took a deep breath then said, "Con's not the man you think he is."

My heart leaped in my chest. What was he about to say? Maybe he found out about his money problems. "He's having money troubles. I know that."

But the tone in Ronnie's voice confirmed what I didn't want to believe. "That's not all. He's hitting on the wives and girlfriends of our employees." He went on to explain the details that I didn't want to hear or believe, but I did.

This news shattered and humiliated me. I knew what needed to be done. I divorced him in 1983, having no idea of the extent of his con-man ways, his predatory tendencies. If I could reverse time, I'd run back to the moment I met this slick-talking man and kick him right in the . . .

Single again, I remained so until 1991.

Mother passed away January 20, 1989. Being a smoker like my dad, she had developed emphysema, which after many years of suffering caused her to go into respiratory failure between Christmas and New Year's of 1988. It was a terrible way to die.

As her lungs failed, we called hospice care so they could administer morphine and keep Mother comfortable. My fortieth birthday loomed on January 15, 1989. I really do believe she held on for that day. On Monday, January 16, I kissed her goodbye before I left for work. She didn't respond. I left her with Poppy, her wonderful daytime caretaker for the past several years. Just as I got in my car, Poppy ran out of the house, shouting in her Greek accent, "Brenda, Brenda. Grandma answered you. She said, 'I love you too, baby.'"

These turned out to be her last words. She did love me; she really did.

The following Friday, the hospice nurse called after visiting Mother to tell me that "it" could be any day now. I relayed that to Ronnie, which saddened him also. He said he would come over to see her on the weekend. I responded with, "I think you should come tonight."

"Really?" he replied.

"I think so."

Ronnie and Linda had divorced in 1978, and he was now married to Eva, a girl I had known since junior high. So they came over that night. We could all see that Mother was drifting away. Ronnie sat on one side of her, holding her hand, with tears running down his face, unable to talk. I sat on the other side, holding her hand and telling her that it was okay to go now, that she needed to rest. "Ronnie is here, Mother. He is holding your hand." I knew she would want both of us there, so I felt I needed to tell her. She took her last few breaths and finally had peace.

Ronal Paul still lived at home, but he had left to visit friends, not realizing Mother was so weak. She died before he returned home. He was very upset that he had not been there. He cried and spent some time at her bedside before the funeral home came to pick up her body. Ronal Paul always got along with Mother better than most. It was as if he could see her pain beneath her behaviors.

I knew God had Mother speak the words, "I love you too, baby," just as I knew he gathered both Ronnie and me to sit with her that night. But I did not tell God, "Thank you." I still ignored him.

I'd taken Daddy's admonition to "take care of your mother" into the deepest part of my heart. But as I kept that promise, with Mother living in my home and demanding more and more of me, I abandoned my children. Wendi particularly felt the pain of me letting Mother guilt me into spending time with her, while both children needed me.

I had thought all was well with Wendi and Ronal Paul. We experienced our share of bumps here and there, some serious, some normal, but we always stayed close.

I worked alongside Ronnie, and eventually so did all four of our kids. In that way, our family unit wound tighter and tighter, in the best possible way. They were my universe—my family—and I controlled that universe well with my love and devotion to each one of them.

I married again in 1991 and built my dream home in 1995. With Ben, I finally made the right choice, or so I hoped. He'd been a customer of ours for more than twenty years. He was a happy, outgoing man, who loved dancing and baseball. Even Ronnie said I'd gotten it right this time.

But—and there's that frustrating *but*—after three short months I knew I'd made another mistake. The business where he had worked for many years shut down, leaving him jobless. Ben fell into deep depression, staying in bed most of the time.

I tried to do all I could for him, but he would not admit that he was depressed, instead insisting he was sick with all sorts of illnesses. I had endured this sort of behavior with my mother, and I had a very hard time handling it again. But with my past failed marriages, I determined to make this one work. We lasted for seven years, longer than any of my other marriages. But when I found him pitifully crying, sitting at the kitchen table with his head in his hands, and my three-year-old grandson, Lorenzo, standing next to him looking very sad and concerned asking, "What's wrong, Grandpa?" that was it. I was done. Like I've mentioned before, when I am done, I am done.

The worst of my three husbands was Con. He was a con man, hence my choice of the name. A womanizer. A liar. But worst of all, he was a child molester, something I didn't find out until after he'd already committed irreversible damage.

Chapter 8

"Mom, I'm Gay"

Because of Daddy's death, I continued to stiff-arm God, giving in to a worldly mind-set. I lived this way while I raised my kids. Ronal Paul, now twenty-one years old and the owner of a condo, spent the night at my house one evening. The next morning he seemed edgy and nervous, but he relaxed a bit when Wendi showed up. It didn't seem strange that she visited—my kids came in and out all the time.

We hung out in the living room visiting. Ronal Paul and I sat together in a large chair-and-a-half. Wendi rocked in my rocker next to us—a side table between us.

Ronal Paul continued to fidget.

"I have something to tell you, Mom."

"OK, what is it?"

He hesitated. "I don't know how you will feel about it."

"Just spit it out." I said.

"I'm gay."

The words hung in the room, but they did not surprise me. I looked at Wendi to get her reaction, but she kept looking at me, seeming to want my reaction. She said nothing, which

45

meant she already knew or she was too stunned to respond just yet.

I simply said, "I know."

I could feel the relief flooding through Ronal Paul, since we sat next to each other.

"You know? How?" he asked.

Wendi interrupted, "I didn't know. How did you know?"

"I've suspected for a long time. I'm not surprised, but I do have a question." I looked at Ronal Paul. "Is this a choice?"

"No, Mom. I wouldn't choose this. It's who I am."

I hugged him and told him I loved him, and nothing would ever change that.

I am sure we continued to talk, but I don't remember what we said, except that we were all concerned how Ronnie and his son Eddie would respond.

I accepted his admission as the world does these days—as an alternate lifestyle. My son was a fine young man—honest, caring, hard working, dependable, loving—the same wonderful son I had always loved deeply. I hoped he would find one special man and be happy the rest of his life.

I find it hard to understand why some parents are shocked to hear news like this. Ronal Paul and I were always close, so I knew his gentle nature. I watched him grow up, never dating seriously, always having girls as his best friends, being able to relate to women better than men. He'd been raised by all women. Me, Wendi, my mother, Frances, Gaila, and Poppy. His grandfather died when he was only five years old. And, of course, he never experienced a positive father-son relationship. Even without knowing the truth or depth of my second husband's treachery, I was pretty sure that Ronal Paul was gay.

Still, I was very naive. I had no idea how much the drug scene played a role in the life of many gay men, and how quickly his life could be destroyed.

Though I suspected the news, it still shook me. I called Diann right away.

"You will never guess what happened," I said.

She seemed to sense the gravity of my news. "What is it?" she asked.

"I can't tell you."

"Now you have to," Diann said.

I took another breath, wondering how Diann—my best friend in the entire world—would react to this news. "Ronal Paul told me he's gay."

"Okay."

"Okay? That's it? Just okay?"

After a short pause she said, "I know this isn't the life you planned for him, but he is still a wonderful son, one any mother would be proud of. He's still that same sweet boy, Brenda."

I hung up. Her words felt right, like the perfect outfit on the perfect body. I needed to hear that from someone else beside myself, his mother. Yet the thought of talking to Ronnie, a true man's man, weighed on me. I got almost physically sick thinking about it. Our family business wasn't exactly gay friendly—but Ronal Paul had worked there several years now. In my estimation, Ronnie might be able to accept this as an uncle, but as an employer? That could be a very different matter. I knew I had to get it over with as soon as possible.

Not long after, I sat down in Ronnie's office to talk—an everyday occurrence. I mustered my courage, "I need to tell you something."

"Okay" he said.

I spoke the words, "Ronal Paul is gay," into the office air between us.

You would've thought I had poked him with a hot electrical wire. He looked totally shocked (no pun intended). I sat silent. After the initial shock wore off he said, "Well, he is my nephew, my namesake, and I love him."

That made me feel better, but how would he feel business-wise? About that time one of our managers, Indian, walked in. He'd been nicknamed that in the Marines, for no apparent reason, but the name stuck with him. Ronnie and I consider Indian a brother.

Ronnie looked at me. "Can I tell Indian?" It's as if he were testing and trying to see if this issue would ruin the work environment.

"Sure, go ahead." I worried as Ronnie gathered himself to speak.

"Brenda and I were just talking, and she told me a shocker."

"Yeah? What's that?"

"Ronal Paul is gay."

Indian did a little startled jump, a few seconds of silence ensued, then he looked at me, then Ronnie, and said, "How can anyone *not* like Ronal Paul?" He turned and walked out.

I let out my breath. If Indian could love him so graciously, perhaps everyone could. As I expected, the news wasn't easy for Eddie, Ronal Paul's cousin, to handle. But time had a way of salving over even that shock.

Later I learned that Wendi and Ronal Paul had had dinner together the night before. He had broken the news to her first. After he let her recover from her shock, he asked if she wanted to go clubbing. They drove together to Oak Lawn and continued to talk.

"I'm concerned," she told him. "What about HIV?"

He let out his breath and shook his head. "Don't you think I'm responsible?"

She hoped he was. We all did.

Chapter 9

It Doesn't Get Any Better Than This

In the mid 1990s, I felt utterly happy. Ronal Paul had a good, deep relationship with Don, a young man we all liked. I had two happy children, a productive and successful family business, a dream home that overlooked Lake Ray Hubbard, and best of all: a precious one-year-old grandson, Lorenzo Paul Benavides, toddling around.

In 1992, Wendi had married Luis, a long-time friend and customer of ours. We all liked Luis—a friendly man who made everyone laugh. Lorenzo came along in 1994, the light of my life. No matter how bad or hard the day had been, just one look and hug from him and I'd be fine. Hearing his little voice call me "Grammy" melted my heart.

One Saturday as I unpacked crystal figurines in my new, expansive house, I looked out at the lake and marveled at my grandson, I remember thinking, "It can't get any better than this."

Ronnie's favorite holiday, Thanksgiving, approached. We gathered as a family in the big house, eating to our heart's content, bantering, remembering, and laughing. I lived for these family gatherings, and this Thanksgiving had been the best in years. I watched my niece and nephew, both so happy, both almost as much my kids as Ronnie's. Our company had a successful year, with most of the family working at the business.

I'd cooked Mother's turkey and dressing perfectly. As family and friends were lingering, then leaving, Ronnie stepped in beside me. "Great day," he said.

"Yes" I said, "We have so much to be thankful for, it's almost embarrassing."

He nodded. We were two little fat kids from Spring Branch, Texas, who took over our family's business—and succeeded wildly. "Life is good," he said.

"It sure is." I agreed, and I meant it. Way down deep, I meant it. But a life of such happiness doesn't always stay that way.

Chapter 10

The Surgery

Ronal Paul was born with a heart murmur, something a pediatric cardiologist monitored while he was young. Now as an adult, he needed to continue the process with an adult cardiologist. So, he and his life-partner, Don, visited a doctor at Baylor, just around the corner from our business, one day in January of 1998. I knew they were going but saw no cause for concern. This was just a normal checkup. Nothing had ever shown up as a problem before, so I didn't think much of it. I was glad he continued the monitoring.

As I worked the afternoon of his doctor's visit, Ronal Paul and Don came into my office and sat down to chat about the appointment. Or so I thought. But, what I believed to be a casual chat turned into a serious conversation. The cardiologist told them that his heart, with its defect, was now enlarged. Ronal Paul needed open-heart surgery as soon as possible to repair the problem. The doctor said that blood might collect within the defect and cause an abscess, something that could cause sudden death.

My first reaction was, "What? Does that doctor know you have had this murmur all your life with no problems? We need to get another opinion." They agreed, and Eddie's wife Dawn, who worked for a cardiology group, scheduled a new appointment.

This doctor had the same look—his face full of concern. "I'm afraid your first diagnosis was correct," he said.

"If he doesn't have the surgery, he'll need a heart/lung transplant by the time he's forty."

On February 6, 1998, they prepped my son for open heart surgery.

Several people stayed by my side, knowing how fearful I'd become. My brother Ronnie and his wife Eva. My best friend, Diann. My daughter, Wendi, and Don, Ronal Paul's life partner.

I kissed Ronal Paul and smoothed his red hair. "I love you," I told him.

He smiled back.

Dawn kept us abreast as we waited in a little bitty waiting room.

An hour after he'd been wheeled in to surgery, I got an overwhelming sensation in the pit of my stomach. *The doctors are in*, I thought.

A moment later Dawn called us on the waiting room phone. "I wanted to let you know they have started the surgery."

I smiled. Ronal Paul and I had a deep connection. We knew each other's thoughts, could finish each other's sentences. My experience became his; his became mine. That I knew the exact moment they cut into my son proved this profound connection.

We all let out our breaths when Ronal Paul came through the surgery perfectly.

But it wasn't long that I noticed changes in Ronal Paul's personality. He seemed on edge most of the time. His moods swung wildly. He angered easily. The happy-go-lucky kid who would do anything for anyone now acted sullen, withdrawn.

The Surgery

The hardworking son I knew now fell into sloth and belligerence. His work performance plummeted. I wondered if the anesthesia had somehow caused his personality to change, because after the surgery, he never was the same person. I had heard of this. Diann's older brother had experienced severe mood swings after heart surgery.

I brought up these concerns with the doctor, who confirmed that depression, anxiety, and mood swings can happen after an open-heart surgery like this, but I think he knew what I was unwilling, at first, to admit—that Ronal Paul's mood change came from an addiction to drugs.

Not knowing what he suspected, I asked the doctor, "What can be done?"

His answer? "I need to run some tests and see if it's something chemical." In retrospect, I think he was trying to tell me that he knew Ronal Paul's state of affairs before I did.

I eventually learned that Ronal Paul's long use of steroids and then his dabbling into crystal meth prior to surgery were the very things that enlarged his heart and endangered his life in the first place.

It took me a long time to believe this. My son knew all too well the kinds of consequences drugs had caused his father and how it affected our whole family. It was inconceivable to me that he'd resort to drugs.

But I couldn't deny the gnawing feeling that it was true. Or Ronal Paul's antics.

After a time of personal wrestling, I decided to talk to Ronnie. We sat in his office, he behind his large desk, me sitting in front in a comfortable chair. "Can we shut the door?" I asked.

He nodded.

I closed the door, still thinking about how I could say such words. This could draw a more severe reaction than our gay conversation. Finally, I settled myself and blurted, "I think Ronal Paul's on drugs."

"You're kidding," he said, shocked.

I shook my head. "He's angry. He's got mood swings. He's not showing up for work on time."

Ronnie nodded.

"At least I hope he is," I said.

"Why in the world would you say that?"

"Because I can fix that. I'll slap him in a rehab center and get it taken care of."

I didn't know then, but that became the most naïve sentence I'd ever said.

Chapter 11

Drugs and the Family Business Don't Mix

Bowling & Billiards had a zero tolerance drug policy. With 150 employees, Ronnie and I felt the weight of everyone watching as my son continued spiraling out of control. I found out later that he started his addictive descent with recreational drugs alongside his partner Don. Although Don could take or leave ecstasy and crystal meth, Ronal Paul, with his all-or-nothing personality, could not.

The two broke up in June, something that saddened me. I liked Don and called him my son. But Ronal Paul couldn't resist the deeper pull of drugs. Another guy entered his life soon. They started living together. None of us liked or trusted him.

Finally, I mustered up the courage to confront Ronal Paul at work. "Are you doing drugs?" I asked.

After a bit of hemming and hawing, he admitted he was.

"You know what that means," I told him. It felt awkward wearing two hats in that moment—as mother and employer—but it couldn't be helped. "You'll have to have a drug test."

To my surprise, he agreed.

But he put it off until he could make sure he was clean. He passed.

Still, we knew the truth. So did our employees, many of whom were shocked the likeable Ronal Paul could do such a thing.

The summer after his surgery, we had to let him go.

I started calling every organization, every drug counselor, every anybody that someone told me to call. I had to find a way to save my son. I had to.

Ronal Paul surprised us by cleaning up and getting his act together. After a long, strong talk from Ronnie, he came back to work. But by September, he could no longer control his erratic behavior and addictions. This time, he really had to go.

I had a hard time coping with this, particularly because it was getting harder and harder to talk to Ronal Paul. What was happening to my son? I couldn't reach him anymore, and having family and business connected like this brought more anguish. From the moment we realized Ronal Paul was on drugs, the family started getting tense and angry. At different times and in different ways, they voiced what plagued them to him and me:

"How can you do this?"

"You're only twenty-six years old. You have your life ahead of you."

"You know the dangers."

"How can you do this to your mother?"

"I'm sorry, but I don't want my kids around him."

"How can he be so stupid?"

We were all mad. I was mad, too, but more than that, I was scared for my son's future. I hollered and screamed in my dream house, processing my grief out loud. One day, I stood on the walkway that extended above my living room. I could see through the large windows toward Lake Ray Hubbard, now sparkling under the sun. And though I wasn't talking much to God during that time (I still punished him for taking Daddy),

I yelled, "Lord, I'd give it all up in one second if you'd make Ronal Paul okay again. This house means nothing."

I wanted my son back. I would look at Ronal Paul and think, *What have you done with my son?* I wanted to take him by his shoulders and shake him and ask him those very words. The boy whose thoughts I usually knew had disappeared on the wings of ecstasy and crystal meth.

A stranger stood before me.

Chapter 12

"Mom, I'm HIV-Positive"

Travel back in time with me about ten to twelve years. As I mentioned earlier, Ronal Paul was called by more than one name. He was born Ronal Paul Britt, of course. Paul was the name teachers and friends called him in school, since that is what his Britt relatives called him (and he spent the most time with them). My family called him Ronal Paul.

At sixteen he announced that he wanted his last name to be Rhodes. Like mine. He felt accepted and loved by the Rhodes family. Also, knowing that Wendi would change her name when she married, he desired to have the Rhodes name. He didn't want to be the only Britt in the Rhodes family. He was much more Rhodes than Britt at that time anyway.

I told him I would find out how to change his name. He went to Ronnie, Shelley, and Eddie, and asked them if it was all right with them if he became a Rhodes. They were all touched that he would even ask and told him that they would be very happy about that. It pleased me that he had done that. I hadn't even thought of such a courtesy.

59

In doing research on legal name changes, I found out that being a minor he would have to get Bobby's permission, since Bobby had never given up his parental rights (nor had I ever sought such an action). This deeply disappointed Ronal Paul. He didn't want to ask Bobby for permission—didn't want the scene that discussion would produce. In fact, he didn't want to ask his father permission for anything.

So, when he turned eighteen, changing his name to Ronal Paul Rhodes was one of his first actions as an adult. He'd always been a Rhodes to us, but we were all happy that now it was legal.

Now, almost ten years later, it seemed he was actually becoming a Britt. This was hard for me to comprehend, knowing that he had harbored a fear of becoming like his father.

I never knew what kind of shape my son would be in each time we talked, if we talked at all. And I had a hard time talking to my close-knit family anymore. They saw Ronal Paul as being stupid and irresponsible, as I did, but mostly I saw my son disengaging before my very eyes. What about the first twenty-six years of his life? I didn't want my family to forget the real Ronal Paul Rhodes.

Oh, my God, what am I going to do? I'm losing my son and my family at the same time.

But life continued on. The day I learned Ronal Paul was HIV-positive, I busied myself at work in a flurry of activity, working with customers and employees and answering phone calls.

"Mom, it's Ronal Paul," he told me when he called. I smiled. He always announced himself like that, as if I wouldn't know who he was. As I said "hello" back, I realized he called me Mom, not a sarcastic *Mother*—the name he gave me now when he was high, so I knew his head must've been relatively drug-free. We chatted a few minutes about nothing in particular. Maybe this was the start of things getting better.

"Mom, I'm HIV-Positive"

"You know I get my blood checked regularly for HIV, right?"

"Yeah." My stomach knotted.

"Well, this time it came back positive."

I didn't have time to process words like that. What mom could? So I blurted out, "What does that mean?"

"It means I'm HIV positive, Mom, which could turn into AIDS."

My pulse quickened. "What did the doctor say?"

"I haven't been to the doctor yet. I just got the report back from the AIDS resource center and I wanted to call you."

I said nothing.

"Is that all you have to say? 'What did the doctor say?' Don't you care?"

I heard the drama in his voice. The fear, too. But I'd learned the hard way, through my son's new angry attitude, that no matter what I said, he had a clever way of twisting my words, turning casual conversations about the weather into full-scale arguments. Still, I needed to say something, needed to fill the dead air between us. So I was honest. "I'm sorry. I'm a little stunned."

I could hear his breathing, but he gave no response.

"Can I go to the doctor with you? We need to get a lot more information. People live long, normal lives these days with HIV." I couldn't believe how clinical my voice sounded, how matter of fact I delivered my sentences.

"That's what I figured," he said. "You're already in denial. Face it, Mom, I'm sick." He sounded mad that I hadn't fallen apart and wept into the phone.

"I understand you're sick, but this news doesn't have to be a death sentence. Let's go to the doctor and find out what he recommends—okay?"

"Sure, Mom. I'll talk to you later." He hung up on me.

I sat there, trying to make sense of the conversation. Did I sound harsh? I was at work, my mind operating in business mode. Why did he sound so nonchalant about HIV—maybe even proud of his news? It felt like he'd already decided to commit a slow suicide, and this prognosis was just another step toward that goal. How did I feel? Numb, mostly. Not surprised, really—but sad and scared. And utterly unprepared for the tortured journey in front of me.

How could I tell the family and others about this? I knew it would sadden them, but would they be compassionate, or would this news make them more scared and angry? My answer would come soon enough.

Not too long after, I went to the doctor with Ronal Paul to discuss his prognosis. The doctor, who knew my son's history of drugs, said, "If you take care of yourself, Ron, you can live a long, normal life. No more partying," he said. Meaning, no more drugs.

That was a big *if,* and I knew it. Aside from his drug issues, Ronal Paul's attitude was not good. When someone gets a diagnosis like that, he either buckles up and does the right thing for his health or he takes on an attitude of "What does it matter? I'm going to die anyway. I might as well do whatever I want." Unfortunately, his attitude was the latter. Although a few times over the following years he would clean up, take his meds, and allow his body to respond positively, his spurts of good never lasted. Before long, he would plunge back into the drug lifestyle, and whatever doctor he was seeing would eventually drop him.

As his mother, I couldn't do that, but my resolve to fix this problem and my ability to face Ronal Paul's death wish crumpled under the strain of one hellacious year.

Chapter 13

1998, the Worst Year of My Life

Ronal Paul's heart surgery seemed to bring on an avalanche of bad situations.

Though I tried to make my last marriage to Ben work, we separated in May, 1998. It was not a friendly separation. A great loss in itself.

Wendi's marriage to Luis had been suffering the last two to three years. They separated that June. More than heartbreak over my own marriage disintegrating, it killed me that my grandson would now be the product of a broken home. But Wendi and Luis did and still do take great care to put him first. I am thankful for that. Still, it was heart-wrenching.

Ronal Paul and Don broke up around that same time. The strain of the drug abuse took its toll on their three-year relationship.

As a business owner, I had a high-stress job with a drug-addicted, HIV-positive son. Our lives crumbled in front of my family *and* our many employees. It wasn't like I worked for ABC company and my drug-addicted, HIV-positive son worked for XYZ company. Everyone watched me; I couldn't escape their scrutiny.

In 1998, my son had open-heart surgery, I found out about his addiction, and I began to feel I was losing control of my family. Ronal Paul and Don's longtime relationship ended. My marriage ended. My daughter's marriage ended. And then, in October, Ronal Paul received his HIV diagnosis and my family really did spin out of my control.

You can imagine my fear and overwhelming anxiety as the holidays, usually my happiest time of year, loomed.

Because of Ronal Paul's diagnosis, some friends and relatives did not want to be around him at all. His drug addiction was bad enough, but now they had a medical reason to be concerned about their children and themselves, not to mention the belligerent attitude Ronal Paul often displayed.

How could I handle all of this? Cancel Thanksgiving and Christmas? Even if I could, the problems would still be stealing the life out of me.

I had many hard and uncomfortable conversations with my family. I tried to convince them that HIV was not easily transmitted, but they didn't want to take any chances. Juggling all my emotions—wanting to please and protect my family, rescue my son, grieve my many losses, balance work with personal anguish—proved impossible. On one hand, my son was slowly dying before my eyes, and on the other, my family was in danger of breaking away from me. My head and heart spun out of control.

As the "party giver" of the business, I always held the big company Christmas party at my home—something I reveled in. But in 1998, I had a hard time mustering up any holiday cheer. Decorating my house, usually one of my favorite things, seemed terribly cumbersome. In the past, I could've given Chevy Chase of *Christmas Vacation* fame a run for his money in terms of overdoing Christmas lights and decorations. I had to keep up my reputation, so the decorating began, but this time with a very heavy heart and without Ronal Paul's companionship. Numbed, I tried to make myself buy party supplies and plan the celebration, but I'd find myself just standing in the middle of my home unable to think.

The normal Christmas tasks drained me. Gifts to buy and wrap. Smaller get-togethers I always planned. I felt like a robot, doing one thing after another, all the time feeling dead inside. None of this mattered anymore.

I tried to talk myself into my normal holiday mode: *You're supposed to be happy, Brenda! This is your favorite time of the year.* But even my own pep talk fell flat. Would I ever be happy again? I doubted it. Ho Ho Ho.

One Saturday between Thanksgiving and Christmas, I attended a ladies Christmas luncheon with my friend and ex-sister-in-law, Linda, at her church. I'm not even sure why I accepted, though she assured me the luncheon would be something I would enjoy. When I walked in, I understood. Each table represented a different Christmas theme, painstakingly decorated by a different group of women.

And yet, I looked at each table through dying eyes. My thoughts crowded inside my head:

Why does all this matter?

Why go to all this work to create a beautiful table?

Don't these ladies know that life stinks?

Don't they know that one year their perfect lives could fall apart like mine has?

For Linda's sake, I smiled and told them all how lovely the room looked. After we ate lunch at one of the beautifully decorated tables, we headed to the main auditorium to hear a speaker. I just wanted to be out of there, away from all these smiling, oblivious ladies enjoying Christmas. I wanted to be home so I could go to bed, because sleep had become my only relief. Except that even in sleep, I'd have stress-filled, grief-driven dreams.

As we stood waiting for the door to open so we could enter the auditorium, one word hit my heart like a jolt.

Rejoice.

Where did that come from, *rejoice*? Why? For what? It came again: Just *rejoice*. I knew that simple word spilled from God's lips, but my attitude answered, *Oh, yeah, that's what I feel like doing! Rejoice. Sure. Bah-humbug!*

We listened to the Christmas speaker. I am sure she did a great job, but I couldn't remember a word she said. Instead, I kept mulling over the word God whispered to me: *Rejoice.*

That Thanksgiving and Christmas proved to be the worst of my life. I can't begin to explain the anguish that this giant problem caused by busting into the middle of our family. Unannounced and uninvited, it seemed to come alive and devour us all. The tension was so thick it was like a fog that hovered and smothered my family's joy.

At the family holiday gatherings, I managed to pull myself together. Ronal Paul expected everyone to be concerned about his medical condition, but his behavior prevented that reaction. He pushed back, flaunting his lifestyle on folks who were trying to be tolerant. I wished I could rest and recover, and then just disappear.

Immediately after the holidays, I transitioned into wedding mode. Wendi, now divorced, had fallen in love with Rex, our billiard manager. He'd worked for us for several years. Rex is a very good man. The family thought well of him long before Wendi paid any attention to him. But when she did, they hit it off very well. They'd be getting married in my home on January 9, 1999. How I converted the house from Christmas to a wedding in such a short time, I'm not sure. Wendi needed me to do this, so I told myself to put on a happy face and get it done.

1998, the Worst Year of My Life

With the help of friends and family, we held a beautiful wedding for Rex and Wendi, with Lorenzo and Rex's children as their attendants. I graduated from one grandchild to four grandchildren in one day, adding Natalie, Julie, and Ryan. I'd known them all their lives, so it seemed odd that they were now my grandchildren. While I thrilled to have them as part of the family, I wished my heart didn't ache from so much turmoil. I know I would have enjoyed this happy occasion much more had it happened at any other time in my life. I did find comfort that Wendi had found a good man, who would make a very good husband and provider. Their love for each other radiated.

Of course, the tension over Ronal Paul and his increasing decline filtered through and permeated the wedding. Obviously high, he attended with his new boyfriend, who had never been around the family before.

When the photographer composed us and called Ronal Paul's boyfriend "Wendi's other brother," he raised his voice and said, "I'm not Ron's brother. I'm his lover." Throughout the evening, he went on and on about the wedding he and my son would have. Although they'd not known each other long, I felt it had been long enough. But the wedding turned out beautifully, and I rejoiced with my daughter.

As life went on, I couldn't let myself fully conceive of the consequences of Ronal Paul's health because I was too busy trying to convince others that his health wasn't dangerous. Ronal Paul told me I was in denial about his HIV-positive status. Maybe I was, since his drug addiction loomed largest in my mind. I justified that if we could conquer his drug habit, we could conquer it all, but even that looked more unlikely each day.

During 1998 and early 1999, I ventured to his house countless times when he didn't answer the phone after a day or two. I feared he'd overdose, lay unconscious and alone, and die by himself. Or I worried that maybe he'd already died. Either way,

Someone's Son
A mother's fight for her gay, drug addicted son

I had to find out. Driving to his house, I felt completely numb, probably since I knew what I'd find: a sleeping man in a pigsty of a house who'd awaken to yell at me. I'd cry all the way home, yelling the same things over and over as I drove.

How did this happen?

He is going to die!

I can't do anything about it!

Will he die of an overdose?

Or a car accident where he might hurt or kill someone else?

A drug deal gone bad?

Some sort of sex situation?

In all that knotted fear, I felt completely and utterly out of control. My son was a man bent on death, and I couldn't unbend him.

All I knew that January, after experiencing that awful year, was that I was tired. So tired. All I could see was darkness. The future looked like an angry, black abyss that threatened to pull me into its nothingness.

All I wanted was sweet rest. Escape from the pain. Nothing mattered. I couldn't play act anymore. I couldn't be the woman who planned elaborate parties, who smiled through the pain, watching her son die day by day. All my hopes for a cohesive and happy family dashed themselves against the reality of my life.

My whole body, mind, and spirit ached with fatigue. Life was a joke—a very bad joke. I couldn't depend on anyone or anything. All the work and love I poured into my family and our business—what was that for? To watch it all come apart at the seams? Now I had to watch my beloved son die, and do it alone. Everyone was so mad and scared, they wouldn't come around anymore. I knew they all loved me, but they didn't know how much this all hurt. I simply could not do this anymore. I could not continue this life full of unknowns, with

68

no guarantee of happiness in this world. *Maybe the next will be better*, I thought. *It sure can't be any worse.*

I didn't aim my anger and frustration at people, I aimed it at life. A cruel twist of fate. What did it matter? Why had it ever mattered? Just when I thought all my efforts had paid off— bam—it all collapsed.

I'm done. And when I say I'm done, I'm done.

So I made a plan. I can't reveal my complete plan. It would be too hard, even now, for those that love me to hear, much less to tell the world, on the pages of this book. But my plan would become reality soon. My pain would be over.

Chapter 14

The Push and Pull and Pain of Friends and Family

W ho were the folks I planned on leaving behind? Let me introduce my family and closest friends.

My Daughter Wendi

Wendi is one of the funniest people I know. She can make me laugh quicker than anyone. Although she has great wit, she built a wall around her emotions as a protective barrier. She tends to be opinionated and strong-willed, with a take-me-as-I-am-or-not-at-all attitude. Wendi doesn't hide her feelings; instead she's direct and honest, something I admire about her. She discerns people well, sees through veneers. She's not easily fooled. I'm extremely proud of her as a strong, confident, and wise woman.

She and Ronal Paul were close, good friends. When he started using drugs, she grew furious and then shut down. Because of her father's drug addiction and imprisonment, she viewed her brother's addiction as history repeating itself. Ronal Paul, prior to drugs, had risen above expectations. When teachers told him he'd never make it out of special education classes, he proved them wrong. Wendi knew this about her brother, about his drive, his artistic bent. When he did drugs, she couldn't believe her productive, innovative brother could do such a stupid thing, following in his unproductive father's footsteps. While their father landed in and out of prison, Ronal Paul had been a productive, honest, responsible little brother that she was proud of.

Now happily married with a child and three stepchildren, she did not want to face Ronal Paul's addictions or talk about it much. Being in retail sales, she did not work at the same location as the rest of the family. And I didn't want to burden her with his daily disasters.

I knew she would be there for me in emergencies, but her anger and disappointment kept her away from her once-admired little brother. I tried to keep her updated, only calling when necessary. She had no idea of my emotional state.

My Brother Ronnie

Ronnie leads with integrity—his honesty unquestionable, his loyalty to family and business unmovable, his ability as a problem solver in business astounding. He analyzes situations brilliantly by looking at the black and white—no gray areas in his way of thinking. This works great in business, but it is sometimes hard to handle personally, because Ronnie has the ability to remove the emotional side of things and go right to the problem at hand. He can be opinionated about what he believes should be done. That is not to say that he doesn't have an emotional side—he very much does—but he could put that aside to problem solve.

Ronnie and I faced many difficult circumstances together through our lives: Mother's emotional unpredictability, Daddy's illness and death, Mother's lingering illness and death, our failed marriages, our childrearing battles through the teenage years, and our many business ups and downs in the twenty years we'd worked together. But no situation drove a wedge between us like Ronal Paul's drug use, homosexuality, and HIV status. It didn't bring a permanent separation, but it did make it hard for us to communicate.

I viewed Ronal Paul as my child in trouble. But Ronnie saw him as an adult causing havoc for himself, for the family, and for the company. We were both right. He loved Ronal Paul—I have no doubt. But he believed we all either do what we have to do in life or we fail. Hitch up your britches and get it done—that was our motto. No excuses. Don't say you'll do your best; get the job done.

Ronnie also felt a great responsibility to protect all of us, and this situation could prove to be potentially dangerous. He slipped into police mode, protecting his kids and grandkids. Understandably so.

I love my brother and respect his opinion in every aspect of my life. When I had his approval, I felt I could do anything. But in the most difficult crisis I'd ever faced, I was on my own.

My Sister-in-Law Eva

I've known Ronnie's wife, Eva, since middle school—a bright, pretty, friendly girl. After graduating from high school, I often thought about her but had no idea where she was or how she was. Then one day she walked into our store to order bowling shirts for her team—as pretty as ever. We talked and caught up. She, like me, was divorced with two children. And she loved to bowl more than any woman I've ever met. She worked in the insurance field. Our business always had insurance needs, so my little Cupid lights went on in my head. I introduced her to Ronnie, who was now single, and the rest is history. She's a great match for Ronnie, opinionated and strong-willed. She helped us a lot with insurance matters and handled all the business trips for us and the managers, as well as all the uniforms for the employees. When we had our big billiard events, she was always there to help. Her love for bowling and her outgoing personality made her an asset to Ronnie and the business at conventions and our yearly trade show.

Eva's interests and hobbies differ from mine, so we seldom spend time together other than on holidays, business and family gatherings, or vacations.

She was a big fan of Ronal Paul, as he was of her. Her heart broke to see his decline. She always asked me how I was doing as Ronal Paul's life spun out of control.

My Niece Shelley

Ronnie's daughter Shelley and I worked closely together in the family business. Shelley is like another daughter to me. She's sweet, thoughtful, loving, kind—and frustrating at the same time. She has a low filter—what comes into her head comes out of her mouth in an instant. As an adult, doctors diagnosed her with ADD, which gave me more empathy for her. She sometimes wears a T-shirt that says: "Some people think I have ADD, but they just don't understand me. Oh look! There's a chicken" It cracks me up.

I felt very much like a mentor to Shelley, professionally and personally. I could always count on her for encouragement, sweet notes or cards, and hugs—on a regular basis. She loved her cousin Ronal Paul. But when he started using drugs, she got angry. She couldn't understand how he could do this to himself and to me. Her loyalty to me turned into so much hurt that she became almost hostile to him, which caused me much pain. I couldn't talk to her about this without her growing emotional and angry. I worried about her, but I could not confide in her.

My Nephew Eddie

Eddie is strong and kind, firm but fair, honest but tactful. He's deeply compassionate, thoughtful, loyal, and one of the hardest working men I've ever known. He is the closest thing to Daddy we have—the highest compliment I can give anyone. Eddie has always demonstrated a father's heart.

Eddie struggled the most when Ronal Paul told us he was gay. He had trouble accepting that, but I know he still loved his cousin. Ronal Paul's more recent issues actually brought Eddie and I closer in some ways. Although he was angry and disappointed in Ronal Paul, he showed great kindness and strength of character in dealing with him and me.

When he had hard things to tell me about his and his wife, Dawn's, concerns, he tendered his words with love, but he always spoke the truth. Many times he tried to talk to Ronal Paul but got nowhere.

Eddie became a strong shoulder for me, but I hurt that Ronal Paul's illness and lifestyle caused such a rift between them. I hated that Eddie had to protect his children from my son. I grieved their absence from some family gatherings.

Dawn, Eddie's Wife

Eddie and Dawn were high school sweethearts, so I've known her since her teen years. Dawn is a very loving girl with beautiful blue eyes and long, dark hair. She and Eddie tried for several years to start a family and were finally successful using in-vitro fertilization. They had two beautiful twin boys in 1995. Dawn's life, understandably, revolved around her sons.

When Ronal Paul's issues arose, her main concern was protecting her boys. Ronal Paul's gay lifestyle, drug addiction, and now HIV status that crept into our family gatherings were issues that caused her a great deal of concern. And due to his drug addiction, Ronal Paul sometimes acted unpredictable and rude. She didn't want her sons to be in danger or have to face some of the stickier questions his lifestyle would bring. I understood her feelings, even though I didn't agree with her regarding her fears about HIV positive infection. I felt a great loss because I feared I'd never be close to my great-nephews.

My Bestest Little Buddy, Diann

I met Diann when we were eleven years old. Diann is very outgoing—truth be told, she's a firecracker, all four-feet eleven-and-a-half inches of her! She's a unique mixture of strong opinions, love, and loyalty. We tell each other everything. She is a safe place to fall, something I needed quite a bit with Ronal Paul's declining situation.

Since Diann's not connected to my family in any way, I could, and did, and still do tell her anything and everything. She was a 911 dispatcher working the night shift, so during this bewildering time, I called her late at night to talk. If a 911 call came in, she put me on hold, of course, but it was great to have her there in the late hours.

Diann adored Ronal Paul, so she felt devastated alongside me when he started doing drugs. His gay lifestyle wasn't a problem to her. The drug abuse riled her, and the HIV diagnoses saddened her to tears.

She would also get upset with him when she felt he abused me, but her love for both of us never wavered. We didn't see each other often because of her crazy schedule, but she was always there for me by phone and e-mail as a strong source of support.

As close as we are, even she didn't know the extent of my emotional state.

My Close Friend, Linda

Linda is my ex-sister-in-law and a dear, dear friend, the closest thing to a sister I've ever had. We had our first babies one day apart, sharing a hospital room. My daughter, Wendi, is just twenty-two hours older than Eddie, so they grew up like twin cousins.

Linda recommitted her life to God a few years before Ronal Paul's struggles started. She was strong in her walk of faith and prayed for me and with me often. Linda loved Ronal Paul very much, still considering him her nephew.

She had many talks with him during this time, telling him that God loved him, and his grace would pull him through if only he would trust him again. Her heart broke for us all. She strongly supported Eddie and Shelley, of course, as well as me. She knew my faith wavered and that I'd wandered away from God. Her story also includes walking away from God. Linda's strong faith and frequent prayers meant a lot to me, even though I lacked both in equal measure. I called Linda often to share my worries and burdens. She tried to assure me that God saw me, and his strength would prevail. She often invited me to church and other fellowship activities—and sometimes I would go.

Had she known the real extent of my hopelessness, I'm sure she would have prayed even harder.

My Coworker and Friend, Tom

Tom is a Christian man I'd known for several years. He became my at-work supporter. Tom laughs easily and has an effervescent love for the Lord. He knew Ronal Paul very well, and had many conversations with him over the years. Tom played the role of mentor to my son, something I deeply appreciated.

When Ronal Paul's problems multiplied, Tom stayed near, offering friendship and spiritual help to me. He would always check in to see how I fared, so I leaned on his friendship and spiritual guidance many times. He also gave the best bear hugs.

This mix of people in my life collided and stretched when Ronal Paul's problems escalated, like kerosene thrown on a campfire. As a mother, I understood fear for children and grandchildren, but I desperately wanted the impossible—my family as it had been before this all started.

I tried my best to reassure the family that HIV wasn't dangerous. I gathered as much information as I could about how you could be safe around an HIV person. But even then, because of Ronal Paul's drug use and his unpredictable behavior, the worry had its way with my family.

I love little children, especially my grandson and my great-niece and nephews. Not seeing some of them as often as I liked wounded me deeply. Thankfully, Wendi didn't harbor the same fears—yet—and she allowed Lorenzo to visit.

I felt totally alone and out of control, which is hard for me, being a controlling person by nature. Once, I talked with a counselor about this. "But," he said, "you're a nice controller. You control with your love."

"So I control, but I'm not witchy," I said.

He laughed and agreed.

With all this as backdrop, you can imagine how tense our holidays and get-togethers became. Before, everyone looked forward to an extravaganza. Now, the only thing in abundance at our parties was tension. Usually everybody came. But we weren't our typical fun, happy, joking, laughing selves. To top it off, Ronal Paul spewed his bad attitude throughout the family gathering. If he came.

The family and others encouraged me to let go. I had to let him hit bottom. I could give him information, but he had to want help. There was nothing I could do. "Let him be homeless?" I'd ask.

"If that's what it takes" was the answer they gave. That advice? Unacceptable. I kept seeking wisdom, receiving the same thing: Let Ronal Paul go.

I couldn't. And the fact that I was torn between my family and my son brought stomach-churning turmoil. I know now that my family was my god. Literally. Nothing was more important to me than family. My two children, my grandson, my brother and my niece and nephew, their children, and my in-laws were my life, my everything. I lived for holidays, when we could get everyone together to cook and eat and laugh and tell stories. Even though the family worked together, when we were at work we concentrated on the business at hand. Ronnie did not cut us any slack since we were family. Instead, we had to work harder, perform better, and produce more *because* we were family. So, when we got together for holidays, we left the work habits behind and concentrated on being together, reminiscing, and having fun.

Except now all the joy was gone. This life, this world, was a terrible place for anybody. I decided to go forward with my plan.

Chapter 15

When God Spoke

fter the holidays and Wendi's wedding, I would follow
my plan. I only needed to make it through a few more
days. On January 20, 1999, several of us at Bowling & Billiards
had a funeral to attend. Mr. Hunter, a long-time employee, had
passed away.

I remember driving to Arlington with Ronnie and Eva and
Leon, another long-time coworker and friend. I could barely
speak, my stomach burned, and my ears rang. I felt like a zom-
bie, but I hoped no one in the car noticed.

After I returned to work, I had things to get done before I left
for home. I could barely move, much less think straight. That's
when Tom came bouncing in to say goodnight. I wasn't up to
his happiness. He immediately knew something was wrong.
I could see it in his eyes. But the last thing I wanted to do
was talk. I'd talked enough. I'd settled my mind, knew what I
needed to do. I certainly didn't need Tom to probe.

But Tom insisted we talk. "Just tell me how you're doing."

Someone's Son
A mother's fight for her gay, drug addicted son

"It's the same thing over and over, Tom. I'm tired. I can't do anything about my son or my family. I don't want to talk right now. I just need to go home."

"You're right," he said. "You can't do anything about your son or your family. You have to turn them over to God."

I had barely enough energy to talk. "I know all that. I'm trying." I got up to leave. "I need to go home."

Tom stood in the doorway, his eyes intense. "You have to give your family to God," he said, his voice growing more intense with every word.

"I know, Tom," I said.

I tried to move around him, but he took me by my shoulders and said, "Look at me."

But I wouldn't. I just hung my head.

He took my head between his hands and lifted my face. He looked me straight in the eyes. "Brenda," he said. "You have to plead the blood of Jesus over your family!" His voice resonated through the office.

His intensity shocked me. I'd not heard the term, "Plead the blood of Jesus" since my twenties, when I went to the Assembly of God church. But something in me wanted to respond somehow. "I will, Tom. I promise."

I drove home crying. I don't know how I made the right turns, how I neared home. Through my tears, I decided to follow Tom's strange advice. So I gave up my twenty-something-year rebellion against God and prayed right in the car. "God, I plead the blood of Jesus over my son and over my family."

The words sounded strange on my tongue, but I reasoned, *I've tried everything else. It can't hurt.* I continued to cry and pray, begging God to help me. "Please God, if you hear me, I plead the blood of Jesus over my family. Please help me—please."

Close to home, I spied the large, white, stone buffalo at the entrance of one of our town's newly built subdivisions. That's the moment I heard the voice.

"Brenda," the voice said, as clear as day.

Was that an audible voice? I looked around the car, even outside. My crying stopped. I am not sure if I kept breathing or not, as the atmosphere in the car stilled.

"Let. Me. Be. God," the voice said.

In that second, I realized God was speaking directly to me! He reassured me that he did hear me, and if I gave him control and followed his ways, he would shoulder the rest.

He confirmed those words beautifully. "You be Brenda. Let me be God."

I'd spent so much energy and time trying to be God, trying to fix my family, trying to control everyone's responses, suffering from Ronal Paul's decisions and mood swings. Truth be told? I was completely depleted, tired of trying to be God. His powerful words settled me way down deep.

"Nothing is impossible or too big for me," he said. "I am God."

In those quiet car moments, God got my attention. I mean *really* got my attention.

I didn't speak my surrender, but it came anyway. I gave up control. I placed my family in his hands—every fear, every worry, every anxiety. I felt a warm peace come over me—a peace I'd never felt before. I wept again, but this time I cried tears of joy. I was going to be okay. God was with *me*—Brenda Lynn Rhodes. God was *with* me. I've never felt so sure of anything in my life.

I felt light, energized. The burden I'd carried slipped away, as did my plan. For the first time in the midst of my family struggles, I felt fresh, able to cope.

As I pulled into my driveway, I knew I had to tell someone. I ran into the house as quick as I could and called Wendi. "Wendi, can you come over?"

"Right now?" Wendi asked.

"Yes, right now. I've got to tell you something!"

I waited for her to arrive, basking in the glory of God. Usually when I called her like that, I had terrible news to share. But not this time. I described my experience to her, every detail—Tom's words, my prayers, God's voice, the peace. We laughed and cried together. I will never forget her parting words: "I can't wait to see what God is going to do in our family!"

"Me either," I said. She didn't know about my suicidal thoughts, didn't know how very dark my mind had become, but she knew without a doubt that I'd been touched by God, and I knew that God had rescued me. Now I understood, finally, what he meant when he told me to rejoice during that Christmas program because I understood joy, probably for the first time in my life.

In some ways, it's the end of my story of control and making my family my god, and the beginning of the story where I allow God to take control. The storm still raged all around me. Ronal Paul was still completely out of control, and my family was still mad and sad and hurt and afraid.

I have heard it said that sometimes God calms the storm and sometimes he calms his child. In this instance, he calmed his child. I didn't know what was going to happen with Ronal Paul or if my family would ever be okay again, but I knew that I would make it through with God's strength.

That night I could hardly sleep. I couldn't wait to tell Linda, because I knew she'd been praying for me just as Tom had. And I looked forward to celebrating with Diann.

The next morning Ronnie came in to my office. I told him I wanted to share something important with him. I told him that I had reconnected with God the night before, but he didn't seem to understand how important it was to me. I told him, "I have been mad at God ever since Daddy died. But I'm not anymore. Now, I'm going to be okay. No matter what happens with Ronal Paul, I know *I'm* going to make it."

He nodded. "Well if it works for you, that's good." He left my office.

It *did* work for me. God worked for me. I truly knew that I would be fine from that moment forward. I had no reassurance what would become of Ronal Paul or if the family would ever be the same as we once were, but I knew I would never lose hope again.

Even as the storm increased.

Chapter 16

The Storm Grew, but God Was with Me

For I can do everything through Christ, who gives me strength.

—Philippians 4:13

Since that surprising moment when God rescued me, every time I read the Bible the word *rejoice* jumped off the page. Like our names or a loved one's name when we are reading, our eyes are drawn to that word in the sea of the other words. When I read Philippians 4:4–7, I took this passage as my life verse. It says it all.

> Rejoice in the Lord Always. I will say it again Rejoice! Let your gentleness be evident to all, The Lord is near. Do not be anxious about anything, but in everything, by prayer and petition with thanksgiving, present your requests to God. And the peace of God that transcends all understanding, will guard your hearts and your minds in Christ Jesus. (NIV)

Someone's Son
A mother's fight for her gay, drug addicted son

This is what it says to me: Rejoice. Praise God. Again rejoice. Praise God always! Let your love of Christ be seen by everyone; he is always near. Don't worry about anything, Brenda Lynn, but in all things, pray and pray some more, with thanks to God—and you will see that the peace of God, which is beyond understanding, will protect your heart and your mind because of God's Son, your Savior, Christ Jesus.

I recited this Scripture out loud every single morning as I went down the stairs to start my day. I claimed it for my life.

Just as I inserted my name into the verse, you can do the same. Try that as you read God's Word. Put your name in as you read. Make it personal; after all, God is speaking to *you*.

Let's try it with Philippians 4:13. "For I can do everything through Christ, who gives me strength."

"I, Susan, can do everything through Christ, who gives me strength."

Here's another verse that sustained me. "So be strong and courageous! Do not be afraid and do not panic before them. For the LORD your God will personally go ahead of you. He will neither fail you nor abandon you" (Deut. 31:6).

Your turn: "Be strong and courageous, Mike. Do not be afraid and do not panic before them. For the LORD your God will personally go ahead of you. He will neither fail you nor abandon you."

I love how God personalized the Scriptures for me after he called out to me in the car. He also gave me numerous songs to personalize also, prayers to pray, people to lean on, and places to go. He encouraged me, enriching me by the kindness of others.

Along with the sweet things from God also came the hard things—God's way of building our faith. He gave me my first test of my recommitment to him on Ronal Paul's birthday. February 26, 1999—it was not a good time to plan a family get together. I asked him if we could go to lunch, just the two of us. I hadn't visited with him for a while, so I thought getting

88

together would be good. He sounded sick on the phone, but agreed to go to lunch.

As I pulled up to his driveway, he walked out the front door toward the car. He looked bad. Thin, gaunt, yellow—really sick. "Lord, please give me strength," I prayed. When he got in the car, he explained that he had hepatitis and was on medication. I didn't start quizzing him; instead, I prayed silently. We went to lunch, but it was a very sad birthday celebration.

I took him back home to be alone in his dark, dreary house. As I drove off with tears running down my cheeks, I wondered how many illnesses he would encounter—or would he even live very long? I asked God to please take care of him, because I sure couldn't.

I called Linda that evening, which I did more consistently since God had rescued me, to share the sad events of the day with her. She prayed for and with me—a regular thing for us now.

"Have you told my kids about the hepatitis?" she asked.

"No, not yet." I didn't sense a rush to tell them or Wendi since we had no upcoming holidays or plans for a family gathering any time soon. Besides, it devastated me to see my son so sick. I didn't feel like telling them of yet another dangerous concern, right now, anyway. But of course I would tell them in the future when the news wasn't so fresh.

Since I didn't share Ronal Paul's hepatitis diagnosis in a timely manner, Linda felt compelled to tell her kids, just in case they might end up being around him. She was between a rock and a hard place, so I understood. But I think Eddie, Dawn, and Shelley doubted that I would have ever told them. I would never intentionally put my own grandson or any other children in danger—and they knew that—but this whole situation kept everyone on edge. It affected their trust in me—something that deeply saddened me.

So, I learned a valuable lesson. No matter how hard it would be, I needed to gather God's strength and inform my family of any and all concerns. I must let God be God, knowing he will handle the situation.

And I did. Twice Ronal Paul had to wear at-home IVs for tough infections, and twice he suffered from terrible cases of shingles. I told the family. Sorry he experienced such problems, they thanked me for telling them.

As I learned to let God be God and trust him, the difficult times became more manageable.

Chapter 17

Intervention

And we know that in all things God works for the
good of those who love him, who have been called
according to his purpose.

—Romans 8:28 (NIV)

By March 1999, I'd been reunited with Christ a little over
two months. With God in control, my life felt much
smoother, even though the road with Ronal Paul continued
to be rocky and hard. During this time, I contacted Christian
drug rehab centers, looking for information to pass on to my
son. I hoped he'd be interested and make the choice to seek
help.

While talking with a rehab center in California one afternoon, they told me about a man in Minnesota who had a
lot of success doing interventions—cases where drug addicts
actually agreed to enter rehab. I'd never heard of interventions,
where you get several people together to make a surprise visit
on a loved one to try to convince him or her to get help. I was
reluctant to try that avenue. I took the man's name and phone

number and thought maybe I would call him and get more details. Maybe.

But as I continued to call other places, I ran into dead ends. I could not talk to the person in charge, or the powers that be wouldn't return my phone calls. I wondered if this meant I should contact this intervention guy. Unfortunately, I didn't get through to him either. I left a message, discouraged.

As I went to bed that night, I prayed that God would give me direction. Which place or person should I contact again? Not one person had returned my calls that day. Since it was nearly 10:30 P.M. I figured I'd see what tomorrow would bring. I turned off the bedside light. I prayed, "Lord, please show me what I should do, if anything. Please give me a sign." The phone rang. My first thought as always was, Ronal Paul—what has happened now? But it was "Mr. Intervention"!

"I'm sorry for calling so late," he said.

"No, that's okay," I said. "Your timing is perfect!"

After he explained the program and we agreed to try the intervention, I hung up the phone. I sat on the edge of my bed with an overwhelming feeling of God's presence. I know God is always with us, but this was different. God heard my prayer and had provided the sign I'd asked for—less than a minute after asking!

So, the process began. He planned to arrive in a few days to meet with me and anyone else who wanted to be involved. I didn't know how my family would receive this idea, but I knew I wanted them to be a part of it. I hoped and prayed that they would agree to participate. I knew they were very mad and tired of this year-long roller coaster. But when I asked them to take part, they were *all* eager to help. My wounded heart filled with relief and joy. I also gathered some close friends—people who meant a lot to me and to Ronal Paul. We had twelve people total.

We all met at Ronnie and Eva's house to listen to Mr. Intervention's plan. He spoke to us honestly and bluntly about what to expect. He asked many questions so he could get a good understanding of the situation and the past circumstances that may have led to Ronal Paul's downfall.

When he asked if any of us knew if Ronal Paul had been molested as a child, my mind flashed back to a time shortly after Ronal Paul had told us he was gay. Wendi had tried to tell me that Ronal Paul had told her Con had "done something" to him when they went on a business trip together to Washington, DC. I didn't want to listen. Ronal Paul was a man; if he wanted me to know he would tell me.

Then I remembered my birthday, which came about a month after Wendi had tried to tell me of Con's abuse. Con called me to wish me a happy birthday, something he still did at times. His words were, "Hi, pretty lady, I wanted to call you to tell you happy birthday."

I froze at the sound of his voice. "Well, you have. Now don't *ever* call me again." And I hung up the phone.

He never called me again. This confirmed to me that he had indeed molested my son. And now he knew I knew. It was probably some sick game he played by calling me after all those years, just to see how long he would get away with what he had done. I never told anyone about my knowing about the molestation, or about Con's phone call. Wendi and I had never spoken about our conversation again—until this moment in the intervention. She told the group, while choking back tears, what she had told me five years earlier.

Con had coerced Ronal Paul into going on this business trip with him. He didn't want to go, but since my son was such an agreeable kid, he went anyway. I didn't know Ronal Paul didn't want to go. I thought it would be good bonding time for the two of them. We learned just recently, during the writing of this book, from Ronal Paul's good friend Bret, that once in the hotel room, his stepfather brutally raped him, hurting him, making him bleed. That was the "something" Con did to my son. I had hoped that the molestation had not been violent, but now, many years later, I know the horrible truth. My eleven-year-old, kind-hearted son, who would never hurt anyone, was forcibly raped by a grown man more than 1,200 miles away from me and Wendi, in a strange motel room with no one to help him. My heart breaks as I write these words.

"If you tell anyone, I'll kill your family," he told my son after he violated him.

So when Ronal Paul returned home, he pretended nothing had happened. He had to sleep in his room next to ours, always wondering if my husband would come in and rape him again.

Looking back, I see how Con preyed on Ronal Paul's deepest needs. He needed a father, a kind authority figure. Con exploited that, enticing Ronal Paul to go on that business trip, then stealing every shred of innocence from him.

Ronal Paul and I had always been so connected. How could I have not known? What did he live through for all those years? I was his mother, the one called to protect him. But I had failed. I had hidden these guilt feelings for about five years, but now I had to face the reality of the damage done. Should I have gone to him when he was twenty-one and told him I knew something had happened? Would he have been relieved that I knew? Would he have pursued counseling? Would we not be in this situation right now? These are questions I will never have the answers for.

I could taste the anger and hatred for my ex-husband. I nursed thoughts of revenge again. But I forced myself to concentrate on the matter at hand—Ronal Paul's addiction. Somehow God gave me the strength to wait until I went to bed that night to weep and grieve and ask for forgiveness. If only I had known when he was a child. If only.

Intervention

Mr. Intervention asked us to write letters to Ronal Paul that night. We would read these letters to him when we converged on him the next morning unannounced at his home.

As we drove by caravan to Oak Cliff, I fidgeted. My stomach hurt. Questions spun through me. What if he's not home? What if someone is with him? What if? What if? What if?

God calmed my worries with a gentle, "Trust me."

When we arrived, Ronal Paul was home. Alone. At that time my key still worked, so we entered the house. Mr. Intervention, Ronnie, and Eddie went into Ronal Paul's bedroom to wake him up and bring him into the living room. He seemed dazed, but he didn't fight them, obviously still high from his last hit. Mr. Intervention looked into Ronal Paul's glassy, empty eyes and said, "Ronal Paul, you have called this meeting by your actions and choices."

Ronal Paul looked at us all, dazed.

Mr. Intervention continued, "We're all here to talk. Your job is to listen."

Ronal Paul sat down between me and Wendi. One by one, we read our letters, full of memories, laughter, heartache, and a sincere desire to see Ronal Paul healthy and happy again. That gathering became one of the most beautiful and emotional moments of my life. As I sat next to my son and listened to my family express deep love and concern for his health and future, I thought my heart would burst. They all put their own feelings and opinions aside and essentially begged him to get help. The love in the room was so strong you could almost see it, feel it, smell it, touch it. And it certainly touched me.

Shelley asked him where his stash was. He actually told her. She and Eddie found the drugs just where he'd said they'd be and threw them down the storm drain outside.

At the end of the intervention, Ronal Paul agreed to go to California with Mr. Intervention and Wendi, who would go along in case her brother tried to change his mind along the way. Maybe she could convince him to keep going—she had a way with Ronal Paul. After many hugs and kisses, they left. We stood in the front yard, sort of speechless. He left! Now maybe everything would be fine.

Everything was not fine.

Wendi checked him in, but she worried because Ronal Paul knew which hotel she'd be in. Just three hours after she dropped him off, he arrived at her hotel, banging on the door. She opened it. He barged in, yelling, swearing, raging. He ordered room service, then drank all the coffee in the room and ate every last bit of food. Wendi watched him, thinking, *I don't know this person at all.* Ronal Paul used to be humble. He used to serve others. Now he ranted about how he was entitled to everything, like life owed him, and he was going to take everything and anything.

His yelling escalated. Then he dropped onto the bed and fell into a sudden sleep. Wendi left for the lobby to call rehab. "My brother's out of control," she told them.

"Just leave him there," one of the staff members told her. "We'll come and get him."

Though it felt strange to leave her brother there, she did. She went to the airport to catch the next flight but couldn't get one, so she stayed one night in a hotel by the airport, then caught a plane the next morning.

That same morning Ronal Paul left the rehab place again and made his way to the airport. Ronnie and Tom were in my office when he called. I handed the phone to Ronnie, but as soon as Ronnie started to talk, Ronal Paul hung up. A few minutes later he called back, so I gave the phone to Tom. Ronal Paul hung up again. When he called back he told me, "Mom, I am coming home even if I have to hitchhike. I am not staying here. Get me out of here. Please, get me out of here."

I knew he was determined to come home. I told him, "Ronal Paul, I will bring you back, but I am through. Understand? I will not help you financially at all. If you stay and complete the treatment, it will be another story, but if you come home now you can't depend on my help when you get here. Understand?"

"I understand, Mom. Just get me a ticket, please." He hung up.

Wendi told me later that she wished I'd let him hitchhike home, that I shouldn't have bailed him out. But I couldn't let him stay in California alone. I bought him a ticket home. Mistake? Probably, but that is what I did.

Ronnie told me later that was when he knew Ronal Paul was gone. His words were, "I wrote him off at that point."

Even though it hadn't been successful for Ronal Paul, I knew the intervention was part of God's plan. I still know that today. God's desire was to show me my family's love for my son—the way they came together, their beautiful letters of love and concern for his welfare. I saw that my family hurt alongside me and would've done anything to help him—the first giant step, in my mind, to rebuilding my family.

As I've already admitted, my family was my god, and I needed to get my priorities straight. God must be first. In all that wrestling, I initially thought I lost my family. But now that God took preeminence in my life, he brought my family back to me, a significant part of my healing process. Some might call the intervention a failure, but I know otherwise. The intervention hadn't been for Ronal Paul. It had been for me, to see God's hand of healing in my life.

Chapter 18

Problem?

Jesus said, "Let the children come to me. Don't stop
them! For the Kingdom of Heaven belongs to those
who are like these children."

—Matthew 19:14

After the intervention and grieving over Ronal Paul's horrible rape at the hands of his stepfather and him carrying that terrible secret of sixteen years, I wanted to have a talk with my grandson Lorenzo, now four years old, to let him know that he could always tell Grammy any problem.

The chance came when he spent the night with me. We crawled into my big, king-size bed and prayed our prayers, and then I said to him, "Lorenzo, I want you to know that if you ever have a problem, you can *always* come to Grammy. No matter what it is or how big or small it is, you can always come to Grammy. Okay?"

"Okay, Grammy," he replied.

"You should go to your mom or dad or Rex first, but if for some reason you can't or don't want to, *please* come to me. No matter what the problem is. Understand?"

"Okay, I promise, Grammy," he said.

I know he could tell this must be important because I was choking back tears, which made my voice crack. I hugged him tight and kissed him once more, told him I loved him, and turned over to go to sleep. He always went to sleep quickly, never moving or tossing around. He just closes his eyes and sleeps. After several minutes, I knew he was sound asleep. But then I heard him say, "Grammy?"

Surprised, I turned around to face him in the dark and said, "Yes, baby?"

He replied, "What's a problem?"

I smiled at his innocence, all the while cringing that Ronal Paul's had been stolen.

Chapter 19

Suicide Attempt

"I have told you all this so that you may have peace
in me. Here on earth you will have many trials and
sorrows. But take heart, because I have overcome
the world."

—John 16:33

A few days after Ronal Paul came back from California,
I asked Wendi to go with me to his house to reinforce
the deal I had made with him as a consequence of not sticking
with rehab. I didn't want to go alone because I wasn't sure what
condition he'd be in or how he'd react to me. I was afraid of
my own son.

When we arrived, he swore. "Why did you bring Wendi,
Mother? Do you need backup?"

Again, he called me "Mother," so I knew this wouldn't end
well.

"Actually, yes, Ronal Paul. I need Wendi for support." We
stood there for a few moments just looking at each other—our
own modern-day showdown. Finally, I broke the tension. "You

know I love you, Son. But like I told you on the phone, you're on your own now. Until you realize you need help, I will not be here for you."

"Okay, Mother. Fine. Just go. Leave me here by myself, if that is what you think you should do." Sarcasm dripped from his words.

Wendi looked at me, beckoning me with her eyes. I could tell she was not going to listen to this for very long. "Let's go, Mom," she said.

I reached over to hug Ronal Paul. He hugged me long and tight, but this was not a loving hug. It was a threatening hug. It was very subtle, but I got the message.

As Wendi and I walked down the sidewalk to the car I told her, "He will either be scared and straighten up or he will hurt himself." As we drove away I felt peace. I knew I'd done the right thing. But still I worried for my son.

AIDS gave Ronal Paul an excuse to die, and drugs had warped his perspective. "You don't understand," he told his cousin Shelley once. "AIDS is a death sentence." From the moment he found out he'd contracted HIV, he seemed to embrace a deepening death wish, and now with me cutting off the supply of money, I feared he'd take his life.

A few hours after I pulled into my garage, the phone rang. "*You will be sorry*, Mother. You will be sorry."

I hung up.

He called again, "Don't you hang up on me, Mother! I am sick, and you just walked away from me! You will be sorry!" he shouted.

I hung up again and called Wendi. He kept trying to call, but I would not answer. Wendi told me to get out of the house. "Go to Linda's for the weekend," she told me, urgency in her voice. "We don't know what he may do or what he means by 'You will be sorry.'" She paused. "Rex and I will go to his house and see what he's up to."

"I'll wait here until you call back," I said. I fidgeted, trying to calm my stomach, wondering if Ronal Paul would drive up, fly into a rage, and try to kill me. But more than that, I feared he'd turn his anger on himself to hurt me.

From what I've pieced together, Ronal Paul took a razor blade and slit his wrists, letting them drain into the bathtub until nearly an inch of his blood filled it. He passed out from the blood loss. Later I learned he woke up from the bloody fiasco with the song "In the Arms of an Angel" by Sarah McLachlan on the radio. He took it as a sign that somehow he still mattered to God. Seeing the blood, he panicked, and still bleeding, he drove away, while Wendi and her husband sped to his house.

Wendi and Rex spotted the razor and the thick layer of Ronal Paul's blood, but he was gone. I wish Wendi didn't have to see the blood, the aftermath of Ronal Paul's death wish, but she did. She called the police, saying he was a danger to himself and frantically wishing he hadn't left.

When the police came, Wendi asked them to take pictures so she could prove that he was a danger to himself or others. We'd been told that if that was the case, we could get him hospitalized for evaluation and hopefully keep him hospitalized to receive treatment.

"Unfortunately," one of the officers said, "There's no proof that the blood is your brother's or that he intentionally injured himself. He's not here to determine that."

Another officer pulled Wendi aside after she'd told them about Ronal Paul's crystal meth addiction. He said, "It's like trying to quit smoking. Times ten."

This helped Wendi put Ronal Paul's problem in perspective. He'd been captured by crystal meth, and the hold it had on him gave him an unstable, narcissistic mind. In that warped way of thinking, he believed killing himself was revenge killing, a way to make me pay for not giving him the money he demanded.

Battling this addiction felt impossible. I sometimes wished he'd been diagnosed with cancer. At least then folks would have empathy for him and would see this as a problem outside of himself. Addiction was a hard pill to swallow for many, and yet I saw Ronal Paul being totally destroyed by it, much like cancer ravages a body.

When Wendi called and told me what had happened but that we didn't have proof enough to commit Ronal Paul to treatment, I was heartsick. More than that, after seeing my mother's similar suicide attempt, I knew what it felt like to see the results of such a violent act. I knew how it felt to know that someone you love could self-inflict such injury. I hated that Wendi would carry that memory for the rest of her life, as I do with my mother.

Still, questions persisted. Where was Ronal Paul? How was he? Did he survive?

Soon the phone rang again. The caller ID said St. Paul Hospital, so I answered, holding my breath. My heart pounded in my ears. Ronal Paul said, "Come see what you've done, Mother. Come see what you've done now."

With a broken heart, I told him, "I'm not coming, Ronal Paul. I'm not coming," and hung up. I found out later that he saw a gay doctor, who didn't report all suicide attempts. He just patched him up and sent him on his way.

I thought of my son's terrible transformation and of what my life had become as I tried to help him. I went upstairs to pack for Linda's, following Wendi's advice to leave. I sat down on a chair in my bedroom and cried and prayed. I opened my Bible and just started reading. God lead me to 1 Peter 1:6–9.

> In this you greatly rejoice, though now for a little while you may have had to suffer grief in all kinds of trials. These have come so that your faith—of

greater worth than gold, which perishes even though refined by fire—may be proved genuine and may result in praise, glory and honor when Jesus Christ is revealed. Though you have not seen him, you love him; and even though you do not see him now, you believe in him and are filled with an inexpressible and glorious joy, for you are receiving the goal of your faith, the salvation of your souls. (NIV)

This passage encouraged me from that terrible night onward. It was an indication that things wouldn't get better but that God's presence would be with me.

Even though God specifically encouraged me through Scripture, the emotional pain I held inside felt almost unbearable. Ronal Paul knew about my mother's attempted suicide with a razor—in the bathtub. He had comforted me after Mother's episode. He knew how hard that was for me. And he knew I had a phobia about cuts, knives, and razors. I realized he did this on purpose, to deliberately hurt and frighten me.

Ronal Paul used to take such good care of me, nurturing me, watching out for me. As a teen he would wait on the back porch for me to come home if I ran the least bit late, always afraid something would happen to me.

Now drugs had turned him into someone uncaring and inconsiderate, who demanded what he wanted when he wanted it. If and when he didn't receive what he wanted, he'd do anything to get it.

Even take his life. Or make me think he might.

Chapter 20

The Flowers and
the Dream

The LORD will guide you continually, giving you
water when you are dry and restoring your strength.
You will be like a well-watered garden, like an ever-
flowing spring.

—Isaiah 58:11

God must've known I needed specific words of encouragement as Ronal Paul continued to move in and out of drug
abuse and risky behavior. I'm still humbled that he chose to
speak to me that first time in the car, then so tangibly through
the intervention specialist. He even spared Ronal Paul's life
from his own hand. But he had more gifts for me.

The Flowers

In the spring of 1999, after the intervention, I bought two
new planters for my front porch. I filled them with dirt from
some other pots I'd used in years past. I watered them well
since the dirt was so dry. Before I could run to the nursery
to buy plants for the new planters, several small, green shoots

appeared in the dirt. At first I pulled them out, but then I stopped. They didn't look like weeds. I decided to wait and see what they'd become.

In a few weeks, I had two full planters of multi-colored moss roses. What surprised me: I'd never had those flowers before. They couldn't have come out of the dirt I piled in the planters. It was as if God sent garden angels to sprinkle moss rose seeds as a sign that he was there with me. I called them "God's flowers."

Everyone who came to my house walked between God's flowers. I took pictures of the planters, framing one for my bedroom night stand. Every time I look at that picture, I feel the warmth of God's love.

Do you know who else thought the flowers miraculous? Ronal Paul. He agreed with me that God gave them to me—a gift we shared even as the troubles continued.

The flowers didn't return the following year, as moss roses often do. God knew I didn't need them again. But his message to me in the flowers remains with me today.

The Dream

Each day was unpredictable as the storm around me raged. As I clung to Jesus, some days became harder than others. One night I dreamed I stood at a doorway with a large group of people waiting for the door to open. I had a small boy with me. I was not sure if he was Ronal Paul as a young child or my grandson Lorenzo. The crowd grew impatient, pressing harder and harder toward the door. I held onto the little boy's hand tightly, anxious and somewhat panicky.

When the door finally opened, we flooded inside. The crowd pressed in so tightly that I could barely breathe. I squeezed the child's hand, fearing we would get separated. I couldn't see him walking behind me—too many people huddled close together.

Suddenly, a hand took hold of my free hand, pulling me forward. We bobbed and weaved around the crowd as we continued to move forward. I tried to see whose hand held mine, but I couldn't see beyond the back of the person in front of me. When I tried to look around, I couldn't even see my own hand.

Although I couldn't see my hand, his hand, or much of anything else, I knew a man held my hand. Gentle, but firm, the grip felt unlike any man's hand I had ever held—even Daddy's. He pulled us through the mass of people until we were safe. Again, I looked to see who had my hand, but I suddenly woke up. My hand was stretched heavenward while I lay in bed. I felt the hand of my rescuer holding on to me. I looked closely at my hand and could see nothing, *but I could feel his hand.*

Then I heard a gentle whisper, "I will get you through." I realized the Lord held my hand. I didn't want to lower my arm; I wanted to hold on to that comforting, rescuing hand forever. Slowly his grasp diminished, but the memory of it didn't.

I can still feel that hand. Because of his hand holding mine, God would guide me through my son's suffering and struggles. And he had my grandson in his hands also. I no longer needed to worry. Slowly, slowly, this control-loving woman realized the beauty of God's control.

Mother & Daddy   Ronnie & Me

Linda & Me   Me & Diann

Bret, Ronal   Me, Ronnie, Shelley, Eddie, Wendi, Ronal Paul
Paul's best
friend

Shelley, me & Lorenzo, Rex, Wendi, Ronal Paul, Eva,
Ronnie, Dawn, Eddie

Chapter 21

The Arrest

We put our hope in the Lord. He is our help and
our shield. In him our hearts rejoice, for we trust in
his holy name. Let your unfailing love surround us,
Lord, for our hope is in you alone.

—Psalm 33:20–22

A little less than a year later, on May 11, 2000, three days
before Mother's Day, I had to have my son arrested.

In March of that year, he had asked to be sent back to the
rehab place in California.

"I'm ready now, Mom," he told me.

"Are you sure?" I asked.

"I'll complete it, I promise. I just need to start in the hospital
for detox first." We hadn't taken that step last year, starting in
a hospital, so I agreed with him, hoping this new plan would
work. He seemed sincere, so I sent him back to California.

But, as it is with drug-addicted people, detox turned into
a nightmare, and rehab failed again—all while I was out of
town. I had traveled to New Jersey to attend a computer school

for a new system for the billiard retail stores. But the staff at the rehab center called me continuously. So did Ronal Paul. I couldn't concentrate on my training while my worries escalated.

The center had to ask him to leave because he refused to participate and he instigated fights with other patients. The staff told me they'd never seen anyone with so much pent-up anger. I worried about those words because up until then, he hadn't hurt others. His rage had begun to focus outward.

Ronnie and Eva helped from Dallas as best they could, as did Ronal Paul's good friend Bret. Ronal Paul and Bret convinced us that if he went to stay with him in Houston for a while that maybe he could make a difference in his behavior. So we flew him to Houston.

After Ronal Paul left California for Houston, I hadn't talked to him for a month, but I did talk to Bret. He sounded frustrated, but hopeful that Ronal Paul would pull through this phase. I wondered how long this would last and what would happen next.

At the end of April, I was eating an early dinner when I looked up to see someone standing behind the French door, watching me. I didn't have time to react, but my pulse quickened. First, I thought it might be Bobby, but in the next moment I realized it was Ronal Paul. He looked homeless—and then it registered with me that indeed he *was* homeless—as he stood there gaunt, unshaven, sunken eyes, ragged clothes. Was this actually my son?

I wasn't sure what to do. Should I let him in? Would that be safe? We looked at each other for a while, waiting for the other's reaction. Tears ran down his face. I went to the door but did not let him in the house. Instead, we sat on the back porch and talked and cried together. I didn't know how he made it from Houston to Dallas, because his car was impounded for unpaid repair work from a wreck.

On the back porch, we made another deal. Yes, I know. Another deal. He again agreed to go to rehab, wherever I chose, and I agreed to pay the car repair bill after he completed the full time in rehab. Once clean, he could have the car to start a new job and start a new life.

This time, I chose a local, three-week rehab that required very intense daily 8:00 to 5:00 sessions. He stayed with me, and I drove him to rehab and picked him up every day. My hopes that this would be a rebuilding time for us were soon lost. The strain of taking him and picking him up added about two hours of driving time to my work schedule. Whether we were in the car or alone at night, he was miserable to be around.

The director of the program told me, "Ronal Paul's cooperating in the sessions. But his anger overtakes him easily. Be patient. We're working through this little by little."

I prayed and hoped and cried every night, while I shoved furniture in front of my bedroom door. I knew if he went crazy, he could still break into my room. But maybe I'd have enough time to escape out the back door while he tried. Or maybe I would have time to call 911.

I hated that I'd become afraid of my own child, but his behavior unsettled me, as it did everyone else in the family. From the shutters in my upstairs bedroom that overlooked the living room I'd watch him roam the house at night. I heard crashes in different rooms while he threw things and mumbled and cursed. I didn't sleep much those three weeks.

I picked him up on the Thursday of the last week of his rehab program—just one more day and he would complete the course. I didn't see much improvement, but the program director told me that he could, so I believed him.

I needed to pick up birdseed for my bird feeder, so I deviated from my normal route on the way home. This was part of God's plan; I just didn't know that yet. As we left the store, Ronal Paul suddenly said, "I want my job back."

"What job?" I answered.

"My job at Bowling & Billiards. I want it back."

"That's not going to happen," I said. Knowing how unstable he'd become, coupled with his continued bouts with drug abuse, it could never happen until he stabilized and proved his trustworthiness.

Ronal Paul went berserk. He started screaming at me, then hit the dash board. "Then I'll just kill myself! They told me in rehab that if I killed myself, I would still go to heaven!" He thrashed all around and all over the car. I worried he'd jump out of the passenger door, but I kept driving.

I realized that I couldn't take him home while he spiraled out of control like this. He might hurt himself. He might hurt me.

In that moment, I remembered that the police department was just ahead on the right—all part of God's plan, since we wouldn't have passed the police station if I had taken my usual route. As I approached the intersection, I turned right instead of going straight to the house.

"What are you doing?" Ronal Paul yelled.

"You're saying you're going to kill yourself, so I am going to get help from the police."

He jumped out of the car and started running across a field. I ran into the station and told the police the situation. Two officers started to get in their cars to chase him, but then I hollered at them.

"He's HIV-positive," I told them.

They stopped and put on rubber gloves before pursuing him. I cringed.

I waited at the police station, not knowing what would happen next. They did catch him. When they brought him back to the station in handcuffs, he looked at me with hate in his eyes—a look I will never forget. I think he could have killed me right then.

The Arrest

The officers told me to go home. They'd call after they transported him to the hospital for psychiatric care. I couldn't believe this was happening just one day before completing rehab. *Well,* I surmised, *maybe now he'll get the help he needs.*

As soon as I got home, I called the program director to tell him what had happened. I could barely speak. "Are you all right?" he asked.

"No," I sobbed. "I had to have Ronal Paul arrested. He went crazy. He's been taken to the hospital for evaluation. I'm afraid."

"Don't worry," he told me. "They have to hold him there for at least seventy-two hours for psychiatric observation and maybe transfer him to the Terrell State Hospital after that."

I couldn't control my crying. I hyperventilated, trying to catch my breath. My chest hurt so much I thought I might be having a heart attack. I managed to call Wendi. She said she would come quickly, but she lived an hour away.

I sat at the kitchen table trying to compose myself when the phone rang. I wondered if I should answer it. Maybe Wendi was calling back, or maybe the police. I didn't recognize the number on the caller ID.

After debating, I decided to answer the phone. It was Bobby! He was the last person I wanted to talk to.

He must've heard my crying because he asked, "Brenda, what's wrong?"

"Ronal Paul's in the hospital getting evaluated. He's getting more violent. I don't know what to do. I had to have him arrested. He hates me."

"No, he doesn't. It's the drugs talking," he said. "I know he loves you more than anybody in the world. Don't listen to what he is saying."

"That's hard not to do," I said.

"Do you mind if I pray for you?"

What? Bobby? Pray for me? I nodded, then realized he couldn't hear my nod. "Okay," I said.

He said a simple prayer for Ronal Paul and for me. His words calmed me, reminding me of the truth of the cliché: God works in mysterious ways.

A short time after talking to Bobby while I waited for Wendi, the phone rang again. I answered.

"Hello, Mother. Come get me!" I could hear the agitation in my son's voice.

I could barely breathe. "What?"

"They released me. Come get me!"

"I'm not going to come get you." I hung up and would not answer the phone, letting it ring again and again until Wendi arrived.

As soon as she came, she took over. She called the hospital. "The psychiatrist on duty released him," a staff member told her.

"Well, he shouldn't have," Wendi said.

"Whether that's true or not, he has been released, but he is required to have an adult pick him up."

I could see the fire in Wendi's eyes as she recounted the rest of the conversation. "We're not picking him up," she told the staff member. "You were wrong to release him. He's a danger to himself and others!"

Ronal Paul apparently told the staff that his friend Oliver would pick him up if we wouldn't, which further incensed Wendi. She gathered her wits and then said, "I need to let you know that Oliver is a drug dealer."

"Whether he is or not, Ronal Paul will be released to him," was the answer she was given.

"Oh, that's just great," she told the hospital. "Go ahead and release a drug addict to his drug dealer."

They did just that. Wendi spent the night with me that night.

Ronal Paul showed up the next day at rehab and received his certificate of completion. He told the director to tell me to pay to get his car released because he no longer wanted to talk to me. "I'm sorry," the director said. "I can't believe the hospital released him. But he did complete the program."

The system had failed again, and Ronal Paul had played me again. I called the body shop, paid them, and then didn't see my son for months.

All that summer I waited. I jumped when the phone rang. Every time I heard bad news on the radio—car crashes, police chases—I wondered if they were reporting about my son. Weeks turned into months during that hot, unbearable summer of 2000. But God had a little surprise for me.

I love hummingbirds and have several feeders in my back yard and on the upstairs deck. I enjoy sitting out on my deck in the mornings, drinking coffee with Jesus and praying as I start my day.

For some reason, the hummingbirds hadn't arrived yet this year. I missed them, wondering when they'd return, all the while fearing for my son, his health, and his whereabouts. Questions niggled me.

Would I even know if he died?

Would anyone notify me?

Would I ever see him again?

Was he in the hospital somewhere?

Was he even still in Texas?

I didn't know any of his so-called friends to even try to contact him. His grandmother, Frances, had died during this time, but he didn't know.

One night as I prayed and cried out to God about my son for his protection and deliverance, I added a P.S. to my prayer. "And God, where are my hummingbirds? Send my hummingbirds, please."

The next morning as I sat outside on my deck drinking coffee and spending time with God, I kept waiting for at least one hummingbird to come zipping and flitting toward my feeders. But none came. I even stayed longer than I should have, hoping one would show up and prove God heard my prayer. But finally I chastised myself out loud. "Don't be silly, Brenda. It doesn't mean anything if you don't see a hummingbird. You know God loves you and is in control."

Finally, I had to get ready for work. As I was getting out of my chair, a hummingbird suddenly appeared at the feeder closest to me, just a few feet away. It came from nowhere, perched and drank for an instant, then flew off. But it had come. After it flew away, I felt tears running down my face, yet I was smiling. I felt such joy and awe at God's kindness in that moment. The hummingbird's quick presence felt like a kiss from God, a declaration to me that he was there with me.

After that, I didn't see any more hummingbirds for weeks and weeks. God sent that one little hummingbird just for me—a woman wondering where her son had flown to.

Chapter 22

He's Back! But Is He Going to Stay?

A time to cry and a time to laugh.

—Ecclesiastes 3:4

On September 10, 2000, Shelley gave birth to her son, Payton. On the twelfth, she came to my house for the first several days after Payton's birth, along with her daughter, Jordyn, and her mom, Linda. Of course, I was in hog heaven, loving babies so much. There is something about my bosom that puts them to sleep almost always.

I was upstairs in my bedroom starting the day one morning when the phone rang. When I answered, my heart skipped a beat, "Mom?" It was Ronal Paul. I hadn't heard from him since May 11, the day I had him arrested.

A million things swirled through my mind. "Ronal Paul?"

"What are you doing?" he asked, like we had talked yesterday.

But I could tell he was sober and *normal*. We had a great talk—a reunion talk. I agreed to come see him at his new apartment and go out to lunch. My heart sang.

Someone's Son
A mother's fight for her gay, drug addicted son

We met the next day. I pulled up in the driveway of a small apartment building just a few miles from our business. He walked out his front door.

I think I actually gasped. He looked great, like my son! He got in the car. I said, "Hi, Handsome," as I reached over to hug him. We held on to each other for a while, both unable to let go.

At lunch I learned that he had separated himself not only from me but from all his friends. He had a job, and he had enrolled in an HIV program at Parkland Hospital. He sold his car in order to rent his tiny apartment and buy food. With the leftover money, he purchased a small truck—all on his own—without me or anyone else prodding him or helping him. He told me that the last time he had used drugs was May 14, Mother's Day, three days after the arrest.

"I want Mother's Day to be my sobriety anniversary," he said.

We spent a wonderful afternoon together. I didn't say a whole lot to the family, knowing they would be very reluctant to believe his sobriety would last. I was afraid it might not last either, but I was enjoying it while it did.

Some time later we decided to go to dinner and a movie one evening. We chose *Meet the Parents*. I remember walking through the parking lot of the theater arm in arm with my real son. I felt lighthearted and nearly light-headed from happiness. We got popcorn, one of my favorite foods, Reese's® Peanut Butter cups for him, and soft drinks before entering into the theater.

In the movie, a guy was meeting his girlfriend's parents for the first time, and the poor guy couldn't do anything right. There was a scene where the family was in a swimming pool playing water volleyball with another girl, who was getting married the next day. The guy, trying hard to impress everyone, spiked the volleyball, hitting the girl in the nose. Her nose started bleeding. She screamed. Her mother, fully clothed, jumped into the pool to rescue her daughter. The scene was hilarious chaos. Everyone in the theater laughed, but I could not *stop* laughing. The movie continued while the people around me stopped laughing. But I couldn't.

Ronal Paul poked me, looking embarrassed, and said a stern, "Mom!"

I thought I would have to leave the theater. I finally got myself under control, only to laugh again. This went on for most of the rest of the show.

Looking back on that episode of uncontrollable laughter, I believe it was an emotional release. We were almost three years into the Ronal Paul crisis—many tears, many emotions, many stresses—when I started laughing in the theater. The laughter burst forth from finally being happy, finally having something to laugh about instead of cry about. Finally feeling comfortable with my son again.

As we walked back through the parking lot to the car, we both doubled over, laughing again—a wonderful night I will always cherish.

Ronal Paul stayed clean and sober for over a year. But— there's that word again—just as we all started having positive hopes, he fell again, never to recover for more than a month or so after that.

Chapter 23

God Sustains Me

> And I am certain that God, who began the good
> work within you, will continue his work until it
> is finally finished on the day when Christ Jesus
> returns.
>
> —Philippians 1:6

God blessed me with strong associations to grow my faith and build strength as well as friendships with other believers.

In August of 1999 I entered Bible Study Fellowship International—a wonderful way to learn God's Word with people all around the world. They hold thousands of classes internationally; everyone studies the same thing. My first year of study was the book of Romans. I believe God started me there because he wanted to warn me about Ronal Paul's trajectory. The apostle Paul pulls no punches regarding the seriousness of turning away from God and going our own way. Ronal Paul created a serious mess, one that was going to be very hard on him, me, and everyone close to us. If you haven't experienced a deep and prolonged Bible study like this, I strongly encourage you to check out Bible Study Fellowship (BSF). God used BSF to help me through the next eight years—an amazing experience. The best thing you can do if you're facing a struggle or crisis is to actively draw closer to God by studying the Scriptures.

Also, during my ordeal with Ronal Paul, God called me to the Stephen Ministry, a one-to-one Christian care-giving ministry for those in crisis. After several hours of training, you have the privilege of walking alongside someone going through a difficult time. You listen to them, pray with them, and encourage them in their walk with Christ. Or you point them toward Christ for the first time. You don't try to fix their problem; instead, you try to lead them closer to the only one who knows how to fix their broken life, Christ.

Two years into my new life with God, I started hearing about the Stephen Ministry everywhere I went, except at the church I was attending. I wanted to know more and see if this was a good match for me. After finding out that my current church did not offer it, I searched for one that did. That led me to LakePointe Church, where I filled out the application to become a Stephen Minister and then waited to see if they would call me for an interview. I really wanted to serve God by serving others who were hurting. I got the call to come in for an interview the next Sunday morning at 8:00.

As you know, I was the company party-giver for our family business. The next Saturday night before my early morning interview, I had planned our yearly Christmas party—the biggest and longest party of the year. This party required the most work from me during a particularly tiring season, and my aging grandma body felt the brunt of it. But I could not tell the Stephen Minister coordinator Dennis Eubanks, "Oh, that's not a good time for me. I'm having a really big party the night before."

I crawled into bed at 2:00 A.M. and tried to sleep. My body hurt all over and my mind was full of all sorts of things. I did not get much, if any, sleep. Dragging myself out of bed the next morning, I glanced in the mirror and noted that I looked like I had been on a week-long drinking binge—and I didn't even drink. I did the best I could to hide the bags under my eyes and hoped I could make my brain work well enough to talk to these people. "Lord, here we go. Please give me the energy to make a good impression," I prayed.

I jumped in my car at 7:30 with no time to spare. Only problem? The car wouldn't start. I never had trouble with this fairly new car—never. I tried again. Nothing. Again, nothing.

Panic rose in my chest. I didn't have another car, and it was too late to call someone to come help me. I sensed God saying, "Be still and know that I am God."

Okay, I sat still. Some may think I'm a little nutty here, but in that moment I realized this was an attack from Satan—his way of keeping me from making a good impression in my Stephen Minister interview.

I reverted back to my holy-roller days in that moment. I placed my hands on the steering wheel and hollered, "Satan, I rebuke you in the name of Jesus!"

In that moment, the car started. Off I went to my interview with Dennis Eubanks and Stephanie Murray, who turned out to be two of the precious people God put in my life when I became a Stephen Minister. They and many other new friends in the Stephen Ministry helped me through my continuing struggle with Ronal Paul.

Some may think my car just had a battery problem or some other mechanical difficulty, but I never had that problem with that car again.

If the idea of having someone walk alongside you in your suffering appeals to you, or if you'd like to walk alongside a hurting person, check your local church or other churches nearby to see if they have a Stephen Ministry.

Serving as a Stephen minister has proved to be both a privilege and a blessing.

Besides my experiences with BSF and the Stephen Ministry, God placed many more encouragers in my path to sustain me through this time. Through all this, He reminded me that he would never leave me or forsake me. He truly would supply my needs according to his riches in heaven—a promise I claimed and lived.

Chapter 24

Things a Mother Doesn't Want to Know

For everyone has sinned; we all fall short of God's glorious standard. Yet God, with undeserved kindness, declares that we are righteous. He did this through Christ Jesus when he freed us from the penalty for our sins.

—Romans 3:23–24

It wasn't until later that I learned the depth and depravity of Ronal Paul's downward descent. His friend Bret filled me in. At times, the news was far too much for my heart to hear. He gave me some details that I can't include in this book. I wanted to stick my fingers in my ears and hum, just to delay hearing the story. But plugging my ears only delayed the inevitable: my son seemed to have a death wish, and he pursued that wish in every possible way. But there is a positive side to the things I didn't know—the fact that Ronal Paul held them from me. Even in his worst days there were things that he didn't fling at me, probably knowing the pain might be too great.

Those who knew him in the drug and gay scene would agree. Ronal Paul nursed two addictions—sex and drugs. He combined the two to be able to indulge in both behaviors.

When Bret first met Ronal Paul, they met through a mutual friend outside a Dallas bar. Bret tended more toward introversion, while Ronal Paul lived life as an extreme extrovert. "When I met him," he said, "I instantly wanted to be his friend. That's just the kind of guy Ronal Paul was. He was easy to talk to, the life of the party."

Though Bret, too, lived a gay lifestyle at that time, he and Ronal Paul were friends, not lovers. They were close, finishing each other's sentences. Bret compensated for Ronal Paul's weaknesses. "Ronal Paul had severe ADHD. I was like his personal assistant, always reminding him about his commitments. He didn't cook or iron—I ended up doing that for him, too," he said.

Still, their friendship revolved around drugs and the gay scene in Dallas. It started with "ecs" (Ecstasy), then turned to cocaine, then meth. Ecs initially was their drug of choice. It enabled them to dance all night long. The place they frequented called them by name. The bartender knew their drinks of choice. Afterward they would go to Ronal Paul's for an after party. They spent two years in this cycle.

Ronal Paul soon moved to meth.

Later, in strange irony, a lawyer hooked them up with a drug dealer, which further fueled Ronal Paul's love for his drug of choice: crystal meth. Since he seldom worked anymore, and I had made hard choices to stop his supply of money, he had to find a way to feed his habit.

Bret told me—slowly and painfully—about Ronal Paul's inevitable solution. "He was a lot more sexual than I was. We would frequent bath houses, where Ron would meet his clients. He turned to prostitution."

Ronal Paul hinted to me once that, because I turned my back on him financially, this is what he was forced to do, trying to put me on a guilt trip. "You and your tough love is going to force me to do things I don't want to do, Mother," he told me. Although what he said sickened me, I knew I didn't force him to make this choice. And I hoped his words were simply threats—not his way to make money. But they were true.

Bret continued, "We felt as though we ran the world. We worked out together, attracting the attention of a lot of men. During that time, we were invited everywhere. Since Ronal Paul was so social and outgoing, we met a ton of people. He'd run at the mouth, talking, talking, talking. Once he said, 'I'm sorry. I'm on a talking spree, and you're in my path.'"

"During this time," Bret said, "I saw the extreme of Ronal Paul's addictive personality. I called him a consumer. Anything and everyone in front of him, he would consume hungrily, like he couldn't get enough."

He met a man at one of these places, who accused Ronal Paul of infecting him with HIV, when it may have been the other way around. I'm not blaming the other man or making excuses for my son—his lifestyle and carelessness welcomed danger. This man also introduced intravenous drugs to my son.

Bret knew as well as I did that Ronal Paul couldn't deal well with people leaving him. He had a growing, paranoid feeling that folks would leave. He didn't take well to any form of abandonment. So, when Bret met a man and entered into a serious relationship, eventually moving to Houston, Ronal Paul felt the sting of rejection.

For two years, Bret and Ronal Paul didn't communicate, until Ronal Paul was in the California rehab place for the second time. That's when he called Bret in Houston to see if he could stay with him for a while after the rehab center ask him to leave. Bret had broken up with his partner and hoped he could help

Ronal Paul. Since I was in New Jersey for computer training, Ronnie and Eva arranged for Ronal Paul to go to Houston.

But their time together turned into a nightmare. Bret saw a deep, troubling change in Ronal Paul's personality. "He wasn't the same Ron I knew, and it freaked me out. He would just sleep and complain, becoming more and more accusatory and paranoid."

"He was completely focused on finding drugs and things to eat," Bret said. "Newly unemployed, I tried to conserve funds. Everything he found in the place, he would eat. I was afraid to let him out of the house because I knew he would try to find drugs."

But Ronal Paul left after a little over a week. "I can't stay here anymore," he told Bret. "Take me to the bus." Shortly after, he showed up at my house on the back porch, his eyes hollow.

Bret told me, "I was one of the few people who could calm him down, but now I couldn't seem to find him. And every time I did see him, he was entirely messed up. He was no longer the Ron I knew."

Chapter 25

The Roller Coaster Continues

> Always be joyful. Never stop praying. Be thankful
> in all circumstances, for this is God's will for you
> who belong to Christ Jesus.
> —1 Thessalonians 5:16–18

Looking back, I can see how we got to this painful place. I harbored guilt for marrying Bobby, who lived for himself, drugs, and the next heist. In that, I didn't choose wisely, and my children suffered without a real father, one who loved them, cherished them, spoke into their lives, and blessed them with wisdom.

I tried to fill the hole by loving my kids enough for both parents, but even that wasn't enough. Ronal Paul grew up with a large, father-shaped hole that I couldn't fill, no matter what I did. He connected well with my father, but he passed away before Ronal Paul could really grasp onto that relationship for strength. My second husband exploited him in the worst possible way, and he felt forced to keep that secret for over a decade, which slowly rotted his identity. And, in all that, I didn't know exactly how to best love Ronal Paul through this crisis. There were too many times I'd give him money, hoping that providing for him would help him cope. Other times, I listened. But I loved him so much that I wanted control. And Ronal Paul wanted nothing to do with my controlling love any longer.

Ronal Paul started off his journey on earth as a sweet, humble, conscientious boy, but as drugs warped him, he slowly turned into his father—hardheaded, his way or the high way. He began to feel life owed him more than he received. He nursed entitlement. And he coddled a hatred toward his father for abandoning him.

Which is why it surprised me to find out that he connected with Bobby well into his drug years. According to his friend Bret, while he lived briefly with him in Houston, he discovered Ronal Paul chatting with someone on the phone.

"Who was that?" Bret asked.

"My dad. We're going to go see him in a minute."

"Really? I thought you didn't like him."

"He's not that bad. Still doing drugs, but he's okay."

Bret told me he thought that if Ronal Paul ever saw his father, he would've torn into him, so it seemed really out of character for him to embrace his father during this time. By the way, Bobby ended up not being there when they went to see him.

As things continued to worsen, it became almost impossible for any of us to be around Ronal Paul. You never knew who he would show up with, or how he or the other guy would act around the rest of us. Some in the family didn't want their kids around him or his boyfriend of the week. He got scary-looking, hatred and anger seeping from him. He became unpredictable, rude, and mean. You couldn't carry on a conversation with him anymore. He would rattle on and ramble, not making any sense. In addition to his gibberish, he had open sores.

Because of this, I didn't tell Ronal Paul about several family gatherings. When I did include him, I never knew if he was going to show up or not, which kept me on edge. I couldn't give others a straight answer to their question, "Is he coming?" I didn't know. He might show up; he might not. "You know he is unpredictable," was all I could say, which was always difficult. Some family members probably thought I intentionally withheld a straight answer. The strain of being torn between my family and my son kept my heart heavy. When he didn't show up or I didn't tell him about what we were doing, I felt mixed emotions—glad on one hand that he wasn't there so I didn't have to worry about what he did or said, but sad that he wasn't there to be with family. When I went to bed after a Ronal Paul-less gathering, I wept into the pillow, missing him terribly. Part of me was gone.

As things progressed, Ronal Paul, who used to take great pride in his home and possessions, started living in filth. Toward the end, he called Bret and said, "I need someone here right now, because people are trying to break in. I'm scared."

Bret recounted that walking into his home was like stepping into a pack rat's house. There were empty food containers strewn everywhere. He'd created one small pathway to the kitchen, but Bret had to step over pizza boxes to get to the couch. "It was so dark there, creepy. I couldn't spend the night."

As Ronal Paul continued to use and abuse drugs, his mental health deteriorated. Although already diagnosed with ADHD, he manifested bipolar symptoms. Everything to him became bigger than life. He tended to blow small situations out of proportion. He took everything to the extreme, throwing lots of fits.

But later, he heard things.

"Do you hear that whistling?" he asked Bret.

"No."

"Really? It's as clear as can be. Right over there." He pointed, but Bret saw nothing, heard nothing.

"You know what I think?" Ronal Paul looked around the house, wide-eyed. "I think there are spirits in the house, and they're whistling."

Bret tried to calm him down, but he wouldn't be calmed.

"There's one in the attic. And there are more around. They follow me, even when I moved," he told Bret.

"There are no spirits, Ron," Bret told him. "You need to get a grip."

"I know what I heard," he said. "That's why I moved from my other house, because they were tormenting me there."

"You never told me that." Bret paced the room. Ronal Paul continued looking at the ceiling toward the attic.

"The spirits and demons followed me here."

Ronal Paul had also told me about the spirits and demons in his house. I didn't say so, but I believe he might have been right. I don't believe in ghosts, but I certainly believe in the devil and his helpers.

No matter what Bret said, Ronal Paul was convinced he heard things. Once he thought he'd seen a ghost. Another time, he swore someone broke in, so he begged Bret to come over. "Get over here! Now! The door's splintered. Someone's in the house, rearranging my furniture."

Bret came, but the door remained intact, no splinters. No rearranged furniture.

Once he tried to convince Bret that I'd broken into his computer to spy on him, to see what he was up to. He constantly felt robbers were breaking in, stealing stuff, trying to scare him. He lived in paranoia daily, furthering my fear that my son was slipping not only from my grasp, but from reality.

My people-loving, "how could anyone not like Ronal Paul" son was living as a recluse, afraid of intruders. My artistic son, who prided himself on appearance and aesthetics, now lived in squalor. He'd sold his body I don't want to know how many times, taken scores of illegal drugs, and nursed a death wish none of us could release him from.

Shelley later told me, "It's my anger part that I regret. I just kind of shunned him when I saw how badly he was treating you, Aunt Brenda. I was scared of him. But something still haunts me: would it have helped if I had visited and talked to him and not let my anger get the best of me?"

As Wendi once said, "A situation like this puts a strain on a family as close as ours." She's right. The fact that we are close makes this disturbance harder to handle. We are always there for each other, to support and love each other through anything. This situation caused divisions in our close family *because* of our closeness. But now I knew it would not create a permanent divide. God was healing me and my family.

Ronal Paul's metamorphosis from sweet, other-centered man to self-centered know-it-all happened gradually, over the course of many years on drugs. That, coupled with my tendency to be the Great Enabler, made for a volatile combination. One situation highlights this.

"Mom, answer the phone! Mom, I'm sick—answer the phone," he shouted. I clicked the answering machine. My son's angry words were the last thing I needed that morning. I was heading to Bible Study Fellowship. I noticed another message. I swallowed, bracing myself. "Mom! Answer the phone now. I need you!" The abrupt way he hung up shattered the silence of my home. It sounded like he'd slammed the phone.

I tried to call back. No answer. My stomach lurched inside me, churning my breakfast. I called a few more times before getting in my car and heading out. I could drive for twenty minutes before I had to make a decision of which way to go— my son's house or Bible study. I called several more times on my cell—no answer. I exited toward Ronal Paul's home and prayed he'd be alive.

Someone's Son
A mother's fight for her gay, drug addicted son

Nearing his home, I couldn't help but look at the quiet street lined with hardwood trees fully leafed in front of little gingerbread homes. What sort of lives did people live behind the doors of those storybook houses? From the outside, his looked just as idyllic—but what would I find inside?

I saw his car parked in the driveway, so I knew he was probably there. I knocked. No response. I rapped louder, knowing how hard he slept after one of his binges, but again—no response. I thanked God I still had the key to his home. I turned it and quietly stepped inside the living room. Dead quiet. The room's odor stifled me—a mixture of the heavy smell of cigarettes and old pepperoni pizza.

I hollered my son's name to the room. No answer.

I passed overflowing ashtrays, my heart rate increasing. "Ronal Paul?" I said again. A large bolt of dark-green cloth obscured the dining room table. A sewing machine occupied one end. He'd told me he'd been making dining-room curtains. The old hardwood floors creaked beneath my feet. I passed the kitchen but didn't look in, not wanting to see what it must've looked like. The circa-1930s home had practically glowed just months ago, before he gave in once again to the lure of drugs. "Son?"

Nothing.

My heart beat faster. I could hear it in my ears. I swallowed.

I opened the door to his bedroom.

Relief. He slept in his bed. I silently thanked God for the rise and fall of his chest.

Though he seemed peaceful, the room around him screamed chaos. I walked around the foot of his bed so I could wake him. More overflowing ashtrays littered the bedside table with ashes, but it was the glass of water there that made me nearly lose my composure. Suddenly I was his mom, standing by his childhood bedside. He'd always needed a glass of water when he slept. Always. Though everything about my son had changed, seeing this glass reminded me that some things would stay the same.

I touched my son, then shook him. "Wake up!" I said. He didn't stir. I jostled him again. My hands started sweating. I pushed his torso and raised my voice, "Ronal Paul! Wake up!" Was he unconscious?

He rolled toward me in that moment, his eyes full of fury and confusion. Red blotches covered his face, and he smelled of sweat. "How did you get in?"

"With my key. You gave me a key—remember?"

"What are you doing here?" He slurred his words, but I could hear anger underneath them.

"You called me twice. Sometime during the night or this morning. You said you were sick and you needed me. I didn't know you called until I was leaving to go to Bible study about forty-five minutes ago. Are you okay?"

He turned his back toward me, cocooning himself in his covers. "I'm fine," he mumbled. "Let me sleep."

"Do you have a fever? Should I call the doctor?"

He turned back to face me. His eyes let me know the rage that would soon seep out. "Mother," he said.

I sighed. Mother, he said. This couldn't end well.

"I said I'm fine now." His eyes narrowed. "Where were you when I needed you?"

Although I knew his accusation was unfair and it was meant to hurt me, I steadied my voice. "You know I don't hear the house phone when I'm sleeping. I've told you to always call on the cell phone because I hear it better."

"Go away."

The way he looked, I knew I needed to ask him one more question, but I also knew he wouldn't like to hear it. "Do I need to call an ambulance?"

He stood on his knees in the unmade bed, flailing his arms. "I don't need an ambulance. I don't need you. Go away!" Though his voice echoed off the walls of his once-quaint home, it was his cold gaze that chilled my heart—his nonverbal bully stance, daring me not to speak.

I didn't.

I turned away. I padded through the smoke-laced house, then locked the front door behind me, knowing he'd probably change the locks soon. Standing outside, his words tormented.

Where were you when I needed you?

I don't need you. Go away.

I could say his words back to him, but I chose not to. He was my son, after all—and a mother should always be there for her son. Even in that, I feared I'd lost him forever.

Chapter 26

Hints of His
Former Self

But thank God! He gives us victory over sin and
death through our Lord Jesus Christ.
—1 Corinthians 15:57

Though spiraling downward, Ronal Paul showed hints of his former self from time to time. Once, during a lucid time, we had a frank conversation about his lifestyle on the way to a counseling appointment.

"Now that you're back into God, has your opinion about my lifestyle changed?" he asked.

"Yes, my opinion's changed. Homosexuality is outside of the boundaries that God set for us. So it's dangerous and is sure to have consequences."

He looked at me for a moment, then looked away.

"It's the same way I feel about any sex outside of marriage. I don't feel any stronger about the gay lifestyle than I do about adultery or sex before marriage, except for the health dangers involved. I am—as we all are—still reaping the consequences of having sex before marriage. I'm not passing judgment; it's just the truth."

He picked at his arms. "But God's love, Mom, is unconditional."

I took a breath, asking God to measure my words. "Don't confuse God's unconditional love as being the same as unconditional acceptance. Yes, God loves us even when we are outside of his boundaries, but there are consequences for our disobedience we'll have to live with or live through or die with."

I went on to explain, "I do feel differently now because I listen to God's Word. I don't pay attention to the world view or the devil any longer."

At the stoplight, he looked at me, longing in his eyes. Like he knew I'd say something horrible.

"You don't need to worry," I told him. "I will always love you. I may not like some of your decisions, but I will always love you." I prayed he heard those words, took them to heart. Yes, there were moments in and through those years of drug hell when my son emerged—my kind-hearted, creative son.

In Ronal Paul's core, he had a desire to create. He made beautiful beds from steel L beams. He created headboards and foot boards from old iron gates. In his first two homes, he decorated them so well, I'm sure HGTV would've been impressed. He knew how to sew, and his taste in color and fabric was impeccable.

Before all the craziness, before he came out and before drugs took hold, he led his cousin Shelley to the Lord. He chatted with her at a party, then asked her to come with him to a back room, Bible in hand. "Do you believe in God?" he asked her.

She nodded, but realized then that she hadn't truly made a commitment to Christ.

"I want to know," he said, "that after this life we'll be together." He led her through the prayer of salvation that day.

"That's when I got saved," she told me later. "Because he cared so much about me and my eternal destination. I only wish drugs wouldn't have robbed him of who he was." Oh how I wish that, too, but my heart warms thinking that he brought Shelley to salvation in Christ.

This brings me to another gift God gave. With all that was happening in my son's life—the gay lifestyle, the drugs, the roller-coaster ride of his personality changes—I feared that maybe he wasn't truly saved. How could someone who knew the Lord get this far off-track? I remember having a distraught conversation with Linda once about whatever was going on at the time. Trying to soothe me, she said, "But, Brenda, you have the comfort of knowing that he is saved, no matter what."

"Do I?" I responded, "Sometimes I wonder." This became an issue of prayer for God to confirm my son's salvation to me.

God—in his timing—answered that prayer during one of the good times, when Ronal Paul attended church with me. Guess who was the guest speaker? A gay man whom God had delivered from the gay lifestyle and drugs! As we sat and listened to this wonderful man tell his testimony, I marveled at God's love and grace.

Walking to the car after the service, Ronal Paul said, "Does God shout at everyone like he is shouting at me?"

I laughed, praising God inwardly.

As we drove away, Ronal Paul said, "Do you know when I became a Christian, Mom?"

Somewhat embarrassed, I said, "I assume it was when you were baptized at Denton Bible Church when you were nineteen."

"I thought you didn't know," he said.

"Well, tell me then," I said, anxious to hear.

"I was eight years old. You, Wendi, and I were in the car. I sat in the back seat. Wendi asked you how we could be sure we would go to heaven and you explained to her that the only way was to accept Jesus as Savior. To accept that he died for our sins as a sacrifice because we could never be good enough. You told Wendi that once we did that, once we asked Jesus to forgive us for our sins and to come into our hearts, we would be his forever and would go to heaven. I remember you saying that after we do that Jesus becomes a shield, sort of like an umbrella over us, and every time God looks down on us, he sees Jesus covering us—the one who took away our sins. I closed my eyes there in the back seat and asked Jesus to come into my heart and forgive me of my sins. I kept my eyes closed for a minute, thinking that the next time I opened my eyes, God would see Jesus when he looked at me."

I wondered why he had never told me about this, but I was sure glad he was now. With tears rolling down my cheeks, I drove down the highway, thanking God for his love and faithfulness to me and my son.

Chapter 27

Holidays and
Ronal Paul

So don't worry about tomorrow, for tomorrow will
bring its own worries. Today's trouble is enough for
today.

—Matthew 6:34

Because family was so important to me, the holidays represented everything good in my life. But as Ronal Paul continued his journey down a reckless path, holidays, as I mentioned earlier, became painful reminders of what I'd lost. What used to bring me joy now reminded me of pain, particularly because Ronal Paul had once shared my love for holidays.

When the kids were young, Wendi wasn't very interested in decorating the Christmas tree. She'd put on one ornament, consider her duty done, and leave, but Ronal Paul enjoyed everything about it. This became sort of a tradition. Ronal Paul and I would be decorating the tree, Wendi would come in to hang her one ornament, and we would all laugh as she left the room.

Ronal Paul especially liked hanging lights on our home while I did the bushes. If one light wasn't just right, he'd get up on the ladder and redo the entire thing just so it would be perfect, and I'd be happy. All done, we would stand back in the street, arm in arm, and admire our work.

A year before I received the phone call that opened this book, Ronal Paul unexpectedly came over a few weeks before Christmas. What surprised me was his timing. He'd always been the one tall enough to place the angel on top of the tree, but for many years now I had mostly decorated the tree by myself. I was used to getting on a ladder to place the angel just so. He arrived at the exact moment I needed him.

As he climbed the ladder with the angel in his hand, the song "In the Arms of an Angel" by Sarah McLachlan came on the radio. He'd shared with me that the song had had special meaning to him after the suicide attempt, which he seemed embarrassed to mention, so I thanked God for this little hint of light during such a painful time.

That was the same Christmas Ronal Paul noticed that I'd placed his caroling doll on the mantle. I had one for each of my "kids": Wendi, Ronal Paul, Shelley, and Eddie. He figured I'd put his away because of all the pain and havoc he'd caused the family. When he saw his displayed, I could see he was surprised I still placed his caroler doll with the other three. He said, "I'm still here" as he patted his doll on the head.

"Of course," I said. It saddened me that he thought I wouldn't display his doll with the others. I will always display his doll.

The next Thanksgiving, Ronal Paul did not look good—he was gaunt and lifeless, his eyes were sunken in, and his skin was scarred by open wounds. People on crystal meth, I learned, pick their skin until it bleeds and scars. They feel like bugs are crawling under their skin. The feeling becomes so unbearable that they pick at their face and arms until they're pocked. He had told me some years back that the sores were from welding sparks as he worked on his iron creations. I believed him for a while. But when I saw him that Thanksgiving I didn't know if he looked so bad because he was coming down from a drug spree or if he was truly sick, if AIDS was taking over his body.

His cousin Shelley has a particularly fond memory of that Thanksgiving. When she saw him standing off in the corner, for the first time in a long time she was no longer angry at him. "I felt bad for him, but not angry. I knew how unhealthy he was."

We were watching home videos, and everyone laughed and watched and pointed. He stood off in a corner like he knew he wasn't welcome.

"It broke my heart," Shelley said. "He didn't want to come over. I remember telling him, 'Come over here and see these.'" It was the first time Shelley had shown affection toward him in years.

He came over at Shelley's beckoning. He sat nearby, watching the videos with the family, truly enjoying our company.

Broken, Shelley realized a bit of Ronal Paul's fight had left him. He didn't curse or complain about not being a part of things. He simply stood away, not judging, not trying. Like he knew his place. "I never really told him through his drug years that I loved him. Not until this Thanksgiving." So she did. And the bitterness inside her broke.

Ronal Paul looked weak, and he couldn't keep his breath. His countenance dropped, his face thin and drawn. He spent the night, because he didn't have the strength to drive home. I let him sleep as long as he wanted the next day. I knew where he was and that he was safe, so I let him sleep. When he got up around 1:00 P.M., he felt better.

He found me in the front yard setting up my nativity scene. He tried to help me but was so short of breath he could do very little. "Why are you having so much trouble breathing?" I asked.

"I don't know. I'll call the doctor when I get home," he told me.

I made him promise he would, though I wasn't sure if he was genuinely sick, or once again, coming down from drugs. Was his HIV situation out of control, or was he crashing? I'd been asking these questions for eight years, never getting much of a satisfactory answer. Soon I would find out the truth.

Chapter 28

The First Hospital

Trust in the LORD with all your heart; do not depend on your own understanding. Seek his will in all you do, and he will show you which path to take.

—Proverbs 3:5–6

I'll always remember that day—December 4, 2005—when Ronal Paul's voice cut through me, the way he wheezed and labored his words. He told me he'd been planning to see a doctor on a specific Dallas street but couldn't remember his name. So I investigated, finally coming up with a doctor's name. I knew my chances of reaching the doctor were slim, particularly since it was Sunday evening around 6:00. At best, I hoped to get an answering service to page a doctor.

I prayed the Lord would show me if this was another cry-wolf situation or if Ronal Paul was really in need of help, and if so, to guide me as to exactly what I needed to do. Then I called the number. The message on the answering machine referred me to another number for the doctor on call. *Okay,* I thought, *now I'll get an answering service.*

But someone answered. "Hello," he said.

I thought I must've punched in the wrong number.

"Is this the number for Doctor So and So?" I asked.

"Yes, I'm Dr. So and So," he replied.

I could hear a dog barking and kids playing in the background. I'd actually reached the doctor at home on a Sunday evening. Amazing. I told him my situation and asked his advice.

"I don't recall a Ron Rhodes as a patient," he said. "Have I seen him?"

"No, sir," I said. "He planned to take part in your HIV testing program, but you have never met him." I paused, realizing how ridiculous my predicament seemed. Still, I added, "Can you help us?"

"You say he's HIV-positive, has a fever and shortness of breath?"

"Yes, sir," I said.

"He needs to go the nearest hospital. He may have pneumonia."

"He can't sit in an emergency room for hours," I told him.

"No," he said. "Call an ambulance. Where does he live?"

"Oak Cliff."

"Where do you live?"

"Rockwall."

"Okay. Here's what you need to do. Call an ambulance to take him to the nearest major hospital. Then you get in your car and drive safely there. By the time you get there, he should already be settled, and they will be running tests."

I thanked him, then followed his generous instructions.

God answered my prayer. He made it very clear that yes, Ronal Paul's condition was serious. This time, my son needed me. And God told me through this doctor, who never met either one of us, exactly what to do—and with care and compassion.

I grabbed my car keys and headed to the hospital. I called Ronal Paul and told him to call an ambulance to take him to the nearest hospital. I would meet him there.

I called Linda on my way to the hospital.

"I see you're calling from your cell phone," she said. "That must mean you've decided to go pick up Ronal Paul."

"Not exactly," I said. "Listen to what God did." I recounted my conversation with the doctor.

"I'm on my way," she said.

"No, really. It's okay. I'll keep you updated."

"I'll be praying," she said. And I know she meant it. I also called Wendi and Diann and told them the same, that I would keep them posted.

Just as the doctor indicated, when I arrived at the hospital, they had finished Ronal Paul's paperwork and were about to begin tests to see what was causing the fever and shortness of breath. Ronal Paul felt awful, but he finally rested when they put an oxygen mask on him. They drew a lot of blood and took a chest X-ray. We waited.

I hadn't called Ronnie yet because I hoped to have more information. But by now, it was 10:00 P.M., so I decided to call. As I updated him, the emergency room doctor entered.

"He has pneumonia throughout his lungs," he said. "We'll be admitting him." I relayed everything to Ronnie.

The doctor continued. "We're still running tests to see if the pneumonia is AIDS-related or if it's pneumonia on its own." He left the room, while the word *pneumonia* hung between my son and me.

Two hours later, they took him to a room. After getting him settled I left, promising I would be back first thing in the morning.

As I drove home, I sorted through my worries and questions.

Was this the first of many hospitalizations to come before he died of AIDS?

Was this the way God would choose to clean him up? To get his attention so he could turn Ronal Paul's life around?

What did the future hold? The last eight years I'd asked that same question many times, but this time he slept overnight in a hospital—not an emergency room—to fix whatever damage he'd inflicted on himself.

How long would this cycle continue? Years? Months?

Could I hold up to the stress and emotional roller coaster as his health deteriorated?

Would I have to bring him home to live with me?

All the way home, I wrestled. If this hospitalization was the start of a long dying process, I could only endure it through God's strength. If this was the start of a new, clean life, then maybe we could begin the ministry I'd prayed for—reaching out to families dealing with homosexuality, or childhood molestation, or drug addiction, or HIV. Ronal Paul could certainly relate to people in these situations, and I could relate to the families watching and fighting for their loved ones.

More questions bubbled up. Would Ronal Paul remain clean? Would his fight for sobriety become another roller coaster? Would he be a bad witness for Christ's transformation if he fell again? On and on the questions ran through my mind.

I prayed, "Lord, what's next? I must have your strength. Guide my steps. The unknown is overwhelming me right now. I need You. Help me. Please."

In the stillness of my car, the Lord whispered in my heart, "One day at a time. Take one day at a time. I *will* get you through."

I knew his words rang true. Jesus had not failed me so far—why would I doubt him now? In that, I felt indescribable peace. I rested in knowing that nothing was too hard for God.

Even with peace, the following week seemed to spin out of control. When Ronal Paul came down from drugs, he embodied his worse self. Being in the hospital, he couldn't smoke or take his normal dosages of various pharmaceuticals. In that forced detoxification, his mood soured. He growled at anyone who came in contact with him, but he saved his angriest words for me. He wanted out of the hospital, but he couldn't walk more than a few steps.

Because of his belligerent behavior, the nursing staff stayed away from him as much as possible. I tried to explain his situation to the staff and doctors. "If you don't keep him sedated, he'll continue to fight."

"Your son is abusive," one nurse told me, "and physically combative."

"I'm telling you, you need to sedate him until the drugs are out of his system. Then he'll be fine." I knew better than anyone on staff that Ronal Paul was a difficult patient, but he was also very sick. He was in an isolated room, where we all had to wear masks to protect ourselves from the pneumonia. And we had to be careful about blood contact from various needles and IV lines because of his HIV status.

It took a few days to get his fever under control before the staff would even talk about releasing him. Finally, they did say he could be released on Monday, after a week of hospitalization. Unfortunately, he was not well enough to take care of himself. He wanted to come home with me, but I knew I couldn't control him.

Dallas experienced one of its winter ice storms in the middle of the week, which prevented me from visiting Ronal Paul for two days. I thanked God for the break. In that time, I readied the house for Christmas.

During the storm, I couldn't feed and water Sam, Ronal Paul's St. Bernard. I'd been checking on him every day after leaving the hospital. I called Ronal Paul. "What about Sam?" I asked. "His water is going to freeze. Do you have a friend I can call to go check on him?"

"Call Bret," he wheezed. "He's the only one I trust to go to my house." I hadn't thought of Bret during all this—he was the only faithful friend Ronal Paul had. Bret had surrendered his life back to God. No longer in the gay lifestyle or the drug scene, Bret became a deacon at his church. Why had I not thought of him? Of course he would want to know that Ronal Paul was in the hospital.

I immediately called Bret and updated him. He visited Ronal Paul that evening, after he took care of Sam's needs. I didn't feel like I had to bear the entire weight of Ronal Paul's situation now that Bret stood by. Of anyone in Ronal Paul's life, Bret was the only one who could reason with him. Bret was now not only a friend, but a personal minister to my son.

Another angel helped bear the burden. My dear friend Sharon, who had taken an interest in Ronal Paul for some time, connected with Ronal Paul at my house on Thanksgiving. She visited him in the hospital when I couldn't be there in the ice storm. She located a temporary place for him to go to recuperate; after a week or two there, he could come to my house or go home on his own.

Bret also offered his place for as long as Ronal Paul needed to recover. On Saturday, before his planned release on Monday, Sharon, Bret, and I convinced him that going to this recuperation place was his best option. We would have to move him by ambulance since he was still so weak.

I wrestled with the hospital releasing him in such a messed-up state. No one spoke to me about his condition. I still didn't know what type of pneumonia he had, nor could I find out his blood count—something vitally important in dealing with HIV. Every time I'd ask the doctor or nurses, they told me to ask one of the other doctors.

My heart would say, "What's going on, God?" But he would not answer. Even so I knew he was in control and I was to take one day at a time. Each morning when I got in the car to head to the hospital I would pray, "Okay, Lord, your will be done."

Thanks to Sharon's help, I arranged to take Ronal Paul to Legacy Cottage on Monday, December 12. I planned to spend the night with him so I could be sure to be there when the doctors discharged him the next morning. I needed to hear every shred of information for his follow-up care.

Before I got to the hospital on Sunday, Bret called me, panicked. "Ron's having trouble breathing. A lot of it," he told me.

"I'm on my way. Be sure the nurse in charge is aware of this," I said.

When I arrived, Ronal Paul struggled to pull in each breath. He gasped. His face, now sunken and paler than I'd ever seen it, contorted in the effort.

When I spoke to his nurse about his labored breathing, she said, "He's anxious. That's all. He shouldn't have trouble breathing." She checked his chart. "His last oxygen saturation level read 98%."

"Have you looked at him? His lips are blue," I said.

"He was just fine before his friend arrived. If you ask me, his friend is making him anxious."

I shook my head, knowing Bret was the only one in the world who wouldn't make Ronal Paul anxious.

I watched, panic rising inside, while he struggled to breathe, even after receiving medication for anxiety and pain. They'd even administered sleeping pills. This was not anxiety; something else was wrong. I thought maybe he was having an allergic reaction to the Prednisone added to his medications the day before.

When I voiced this to the nurse on duty, she said, "It's not likely. He's actually been on that several days."

Ronal Paul could not lie down. He couldn't keep still. He gasped, broke out in sweats, then flushed red. His body shook. He sunk into delirium, seeing dogs, cats, and rats. He reached for things or people that were not there. In every possible way, he begged for help.

Not being able to breathe will do that to a person.

Chapter 29

If You Weren't
Already in a Hospital,
I'd Call 911

For we live by believing and not by seeing.
—2 Corinthians 5:7

I called for the exiting nurse to look at Ronal Paul ten minutes
before her shift ended. But the shift change passed—still no
nurse. Almost midnight now, I went to the nurse's station, only
to find the nurse casually speaking to someone.

I didn't care what she thought. I hollered, "Something is
wrong! This isn't just anxiety. None of the meds work, though
they have been working all week to give him temporary relief."

She pulled me aside. "Maybe you are upsetting him. All his
vitals are fine. Do I need to remind you that his oxygen levels
were 98%?" She rolled her eyes. "He is only anxious."

I shook my head. "I don't care what the reading says, ma'am.
Something is not right. Please do something."

Eventually, she called the doctor on duty, who ordered more
meds for anxiety—which of course did not work.

A new nurse started the 11:00—7:00 shift. Like a skipped record from my childhood, he repeated the same news: Ronal Paul was anxious. Nothing more.

At one point, the nurse tried to get a reading on his oxygen saturation level with a hand-held reader, but it didn't work. He attempted this twice. "I'm sorry. The machine's not working," he said. "You need to talk to the respiratory technician. She'll take his levels when she gives the patient his breathing treatment."

When she arrived, I asked her to please check his oxygen levels.

"I'll be right back," she said. But she never returned.

Ronal Paul struggled to form his words, but when he did, he said, "I can't breathe." Every time he said that, I called the nurses' station. "We are still struggling here! We need something done!" Either we'd have no response, or a nurse would enter the room, say a quick, "It's anxiety," and leave us alone with Ronal Paul's rasping, desperate breaths.

Ronal Paul could not get to the bathroom when he needed to, so he soiled his clothes during that long night. He sat, slumped, on the side of the bed, gasping, all the while reaching for me. I tried to comfort him.

"Mom," he said. "You need to lie down and rest." He pointed to the bed he couldn't recline in. His words salved my heart. For the first time in I didn't know how long, he showed concern for me. One of the first things drugs had robbed from my son was his deep sense of empathy and care, and now I experienced it while he experienced so much pain and suffering. He was finally getting clear-headed, but suffering terribly. As bad as the night was, we bonded once again. I thanked God for that.

The next morning at 9:00, the day they were supposed to discharge him, a young girl came in from Respiratory to give Ronal Paul a breathing treatment. She checked his oxygen level immediately, then looked at me with panic in her eyes.

"Has he had his oxygen on during the night?" she asked.

"Yes," I said. "All night long."

She shook her head.

I swallowed. "What is his oxygen level?"

"Very low. Are you sure you had his oxygen turned on?"

"Completely sure. I've been here all night. Is something wrong with the oxygen?"

She measured Ronal Paul's level again. "It's below fifty," she said. She immediately called someone into the room.

My son continued to fight for breath. With a level so low, I realized this was not an allergic reaction to Prednisone. He had some sort of physical problem—one ignored for the last eighteen hours!

Another person from respiratory arrived and went to work immediately to resolve the situation. He placed a mask on Ronal Paul and added a monitor to read his levels. His oxygen levels increased from fifty to ninety, and his heart rate lowered from 150 to 120. The technician had to put a stronger mask on Ronal Paul to keep his oxygen level above ninety. He paged the doctor on call and ordered a chest X-ray.

I thanked God for those two respiratory therapists, who rescued my son. But I struggled to understand his nurses, who seemed unconcerned. They could've allowed him to die.

Finally Ronal Paul slept.

When radiology came in to do a chest X-ray, I stepped out into the hall to call Wendi and recount the night's ordeal. I didn't ask her to come to the hospital because I knew she couldn't handle much more. She visited during the week, but afterward she said, "I'm sorry, Mom, but I can't take this. He is mean. He is not my brother anymore. I know he's sick, but he's too much like Dad right now. I just don't want to go there."

"I understand." I shook my head, "He was so good for twenty-six years." I said.

"I know. We had a good run for twenty-six years, I guess," she had said.

So, knowing how she felt, we exchanged "I love yous" and hung up, while tears ran down my face.

I went back into Ronal Paul's room. He slept soundly, a tight mask forcing much-needed oxygen into his lungs. I stretched out on the recliner to rest. After a nap, I heard the door open. Wendi! We hugged and cried. She looked at her little brother lying there with his eyes half open and rolled back in his head, finally resting from exhaustion.

The doctor entered shortly after our reunion.

"I have the results. His right lung is significantly collapsed." He looked at Ronal Paul. "This is not unusual with pneumonia patients."

Fed up, I said, "You'd think medical professionals would know to look for that then. If a pneumonia patient suddenly couldn't breathe, you'd think they'd pay attention. Do you realize that he suffered for eighteen hours like this?"

He apologized.

"What do we do now?" Wendi asked.

"He needs a surgical procedure to re-inflate the lung. Then he will spend several days in ICU so he can be closely monitored."

"I guess he won't be discharged today?" I asked, not tempering my sarcasm.

"No. He'll need to be here several more days." He left the room.

Soon after, a very nice young doctor came in to do the procedure right there in the room. "You're welcome to stay," he told us.

We did.

He explained everything as he went along, full of compassion for Ronal Paul and us. I noticed the Christian fish symbol on his name tag, which comforted me. The doctor was in his early thirties like Ronal Paul, about his size, nice-looking, with red hair. I couldn't help but compare both lives, both sets of choices that had led to this moment. One young man a fine doctor, the other a drug addict with AIDS. My son, the drug addict with AIDS. How did this happen?

The doctor made an incision and inserted the tube into my son's chest wall so fluid could drain out to make room for the lung to re-inflate—all this while Ronal Paul rested. Linda visited for several hours. Bret, too. Ronnie, Eva, and Indian came in the evening until the staff moved Ronal Paul to ICU. I couldn't go in to ICU with him, so I took my tired self home. Another ride home of crying and praying, "What's happening, God?"

"I am with you," he answered.

Since I couldn't visit as much with Ronal Paul in ICU, I had a little more time to prepare for Christmas—just weeks away and I wasn't nearly ready. Surely he would be out of the hospital in plenty of time for Christmas. I wondered if he'd be well enough physically and mentally to be at my house for the holidays. In between preparations, I drove to the hospital to visit Ronal Paul during the two allotted visiting slots, and I stayed in the waiting room between visits.

I addressed my Christmas cards there. I included a personal note in the card I sent to my cousin, Larry Rhodes, in Illinois, asking him to please pray for Ronal Paul in the hospital with pneumonia.

Larry is our family minister, conducting most of the weddings and funerals for cousins, aunts, and uncles. I always enjoyed our times together but never had enough time to get really close. He married Wendi and her first husband, Luis, me and my third husband, and conducted the funerals for Daddy and Mother. He made me blush at our Aunt Ora Lee's funeral when he said, "I enjoy being the family minister. The only problem is those I bury stay buried better than those I marry stay married."

A few days after mailing my Christmas cards, Larry called. I updated him on Ronal Paul's prognosis.

"How are you holding up?" he asked.

"Okay," I said. "But the hard part is not knowing what lies ahead. Is this the first of many hospitalizations or is this what it will take to turn his life around?"

"No one can say that for certain. But you must prepare your heart for anything."

"I know God is in control. I think I'm prepared for anything. Even if he doesn't survive this." The words came from my mouth in such a nonchalant way, they surprised me. I truly hadn't given death a serious thought through this ordeal. The doctors hadn't given me any indication that he was that ill.

Larry cleared his throat. "Are you prepared if he doesn't survive this?"

"I don't think that's going to happen," I told him, "but I have lived with that possibility for eight years now, never knowing what was going to happen next."

"Well, you know Laura and I will be praying for you. Please keep me posted," he said.

I felt better after hearing from him.

But Ronal Paul's attitude continued to be difficult in ICU. He wanted out of the hospital, but he couldn't leave, so he took it out on me. After one particularly disrespectful exchange, I decided I wouldn't take his mouthy ways anymore. "You are not going to treat me that way," I told him. "I'm doing everything possible to help you. I do not deserve to be talked to like that." I walked out of the room.

I stayed in the waiting room three hours until the next visiting time. When I returned, he reached for me.

"Mom," he said. "Please come here."

I took his hand.

"I'm sorry. I don't mean to sound so mean. I don't know what I'd do without you. I just want out of here."

"I know, Son, but you have to get better first. There's no reason to talk to me or the nurses like that. I know you feel awful, but we're all trying to help you."

"I know, Mom. I'll try."

We hugged and exchanged "I love yous."

One of Ronal Paul's problems throughout the years was his insistence on self-medication for various psychological issues. Doctors diagnosed him as bipolar and with social anxiety disorder, ADD, and depression. He abused the prescribed medications for years, bouncing from one doctor to the next, receiving more and different medications, taking them in abundance. Now hospitalized and given regimented, appropriate levels of medication, the proper amounts were not enough for him.

The doctor told me Thursday that Ronal Paul's lung wouldn't re-inflate due to a leak. Because of this, they couldn't safely remove the pump or tubing. "He'll need to stay in ICU a few more days," the doctor said. "Our hope is that the leak will heal itself." But by Saturday, December 17, the leak hadn't healed. They moved him back to the floor against my wishes.

I insisted they put him close to the nurse's station for close observation. No longer in isolation since his fever left, he still wore an oxygen mask, and he was attached to several IV lines and a chest pump. But his care level dropped. And the hole in his lung didn't heal.

On Monday, the doctor came into the room. "I'm calling in a surgeon to operate on the lung to find the leak and repair it surgically."

"Does that mean you're opening his chest?"

"You'll have to ask the surgeon when he comes in later," he said.

I stayed all day Monday until late into the night. I returned early Tuesday so I wouldn't miss seeing the surgeon.

While waiting, Ronal Paul said, "Mom, I don't want to stay here."

"What do you mean? You know you can't be released now."

"I want to change hospitals. Please."

"Where do you want to go?"

"I don't know. I hate this place."

"I do, too. Let's see what the surgeon says and then decide. If we leave here, we'll go to Medical City."

"Okay," he said. I thought he was going to cry. "That would be great, Mom."

This was the first decent conversation we'd had in two years. He was almost like his old self again.

I called my niece-in-law, Dawn, Eddie's wife, who worked for pulmonary doctors at Medical City. I asked her about getting him transferred. She made calls, securing a doctor to take Ronal Paul's case if we relocated.

The surgeon finally came in late Tuesday afternoon. He looked at the chest pump and said, "I'll be scheduling surgery tomorrow at 2:00 P.M." He started to leave the room, not having even touched Ronal Paul.

"Wait," I said.

He turned, stood in the doorway.

"What is involved with the surgery? Do you have to open the chest?"

"If I can't find the leak any other way, that's a possibility."

Ronal Paul and I looked at each other, each knowing what the other was thinking. I knew at that point that we weren't going to let this indifferent man open his chest. We were finished with this hospital.

"I want to move him to another hospital. Can he be moved safely?"

The doctor looked surprised, then said, "In an ambulance."

"What do I need to do to get him moved?"

He shook his head. "If you want to move him in his condition, that's your right, ma'am. Talk to the nurses' station."

Chapter 30

A New Hospital

> Dear brothers and sisters, when troubles come your
> way, consider it an opportunity for great joy. For
> you know that when your faith is tested, your en-
> durance has a chance to grow.
>
> —James 1:2–3

So I initiated the transfer process, enduring twenty-
four hours of dirty looks from the staff. At 4:00 P.M.,
Wednesday, December 21, the ambulance took Ronal Paul to
Medical City, the place he'd received his heart surgery so many
years before. I thanked God we could get him to a better place.

The open-heart surgery at Medical City in 1998 had seemed
to initiate his downward spiral. Would this stay end it? And if
it did, how? Death? Or transformation?

I drove my car, but not together with the ambulance, since
we couldn't park in the same area. I knew his room number. I
hoped to get to his room so I could welcome him into his new
environment. As I got off the elevator to find his room, the
paramedics wheeled him down the hall toward me. I thanked
God for this little coincidence.

Someone's Son
A mother's fight for her gay, drug addicted son

Being in the new hospital felt like we'd been released from prison and now relocated to a resort. Ronal Paul's first words in the new room made me smile. "Look, Mom," he said. "I actually have a view. And pictures on the walls." He pointed to the floor. "It's hardwood." For my aesthetically bent son, having a corner room with a view, tastefully decorated, blessed him.

It was like God had given him a big spanking, sobering him up in the first hospital, before giving him a hug by bringing him to Medical City.

Immediately, the medical staff introduced themselves, then took his vitals. We noticed how compassionately they dealt with us, and we rejoiced that each piece of medical equipment worked. A nurse placed a monitor on his finger to read his oxygen level at *all* times. I took a deep breath of relief and thanked God for his provisions—my niece-in-law Dawn being one of them.

In less than thirty minutes, the infectious-disease doctor on staff introduced himself. He asked many questions and answered many of ours. "A pulmonary specialist will see you tomorrow," he said. "They'll read all his records from the previous hospital and discuss treatment as soon as possible." Unhurried, he stayed as long as we asked questions, something I appreciated after Ronal Paul's two-and-a-half weeks in the other hospital.

Now settled, Ronal Paul seemed to come back to himself. "I'm hungry," he said. "I want Campisi's pizza."

I called Bret, told him our new location—just a few blocks from his apartment, and asked if he could bring the pizza.

That evening the extended family planned to attend a Christmas program. Initially, I told everyone I couldn't attend. But now with Ronal Paul in good hands, I decided to go. It felt great to be out, to spend a relaxing evening with my family. On the way home, with Lorenzo and Natalie in tow, I decided to check on Ronal Paul, hoping to find him sleeping.

A New Hospital

Unfortunately, he was not only awake, but he wasn't breathing well. This made him mad. He chose to take his frustration out on me, in front of the grandkids. I did my best to get him settled down, then I talked to the nurse. Would this roller coaster ever end?

I couldn't stay; I had to take the kids home. I felt awful they had seen him rude and hateful to me, but as we left Natalie tugged at my sleeve. "That's okay, Grammy," she said. "Sometimes when you feel really bad, you take it out on the one you love the most."

Through blurry eyes I said, "That's very true, Sweetie. Thanks for understanding. Both of you know that he loves me even when he doesn't show it, right?"

They both nodded yes. The car ride stayed quiet the rest of the way home.

The next day, December 22, the pulmonary specialist planned a lung biopsy to know Ronal Paul's exact condition.

Around midday, while Ronnie, Eva, and Bret visited, Ronal Paul started crying.

I went to his side and said, "What's wrong, Son?"

"I don't want to die like this."

What? I thought. *Die? No one said you were dying. You are not dying.* What I said: "I don't think you are going to die, Son. But you know that you don't have to die like this, right?"

"I know," he said. "No more drugs. No more smoking. I'm going to take much better care of myself when I get out of here."

Behind my back, toward Ronnie and Eva, I gave a thumbs-up sign. Bret later told me Ronal Paul had cried off and on since he got there that morning, and that they'd been praying together—the breakthrough I'd prayed for the past several years. He needed to take responsibility for his actions and turn away from them and back to God—a necessary and important first step.

Someone's Son
A mother's fight for her gay, drug addicted son

My thoughts swirled around me. *Even if he fails again, he has to take this first step toward recovery. Today is a much better day. His attitude will improve, and hopefully his health will follow.*

Ronnie and Eva encouraged him before they left. I walked them out, chattering with joy. "It's such a relief," I said. "He's finally showing remorse for his past mistakes. It's a start." We hugged, then they left.

If it took a scare this severe, then so be it. But as I walked back to Ronal Paul's room, fear took hold again. As a mom, I longed for a full recovery—physically, emotionally, and spiritually, but I doubted if I had the wherewithal to handle more failures, more battles. I knew most alcoholics and drug addicts failed more than once before achieving true sobriety. What I needed: God's strength. And a miracle.

When I returned, a staff person wheeled Ronal Paul out to do the lung biopsy, saying it would take about two hours. The doctor would deliver his findings as soon as they finished.

Bret and I walked downstairs to get lunch. We talked about Ronal Paul's new life after this hospital stay, dreaming of a drug-free son and friend. After our conversation, Bret decided to go home, then come back in the evening. I returned to Ronal Paul's room. I called Linda, Wendi, and Diann to share the good news while I waited for the doctor. All three rejoiced with me, but cautioned me to not get my hopes up too high.

So I waited. The phone rang. I figured it must be a friend or relative checking in.

"Hello," a man said. "Is this Ron Rhodes' mother?"

"Yes, this is Brenda Rhodes."

"This is Dr. S. I'm finished with the lung biopsy."

"How did it go?" I ask, feeling upbeat.

The doctor paused. "He is very sick," he said.

"Yes, sir," I said with a question in my voice.

"Ma'am, I'm worried he may not survive."

"What do you mean?" I sat on Ronal Paul's empty bed. My heart rate elevated.

"His lungs are very diseased," he said. "I'm concerned he may not *survive*." This time he emphasized the word survive, drawing it out a bit.

My throat constricted. "This illness? You think he may not survive this illness?" My voice cracked.

"Yes, that's correct. I hope I am wrong. I hate to have to tell you this by phone. I'll be up to talk to you later this evening."

I'm not sure how I had the state of mind to ask him, but I remembered the leak in his lung. "What about the leak? Are you going to operate on that?"

"No. His lungs are too weak to operate. I would never cut into lungs this diseased."

Oh, dear God, I thought.

"Your son has little or no resistance right now. AIDS has advanced to a critical stage. His condition is most likely terminal. I'm so sorry." He spoke with remorse and care. A man I'd never met delivered the most painful news of my life. I could barely absorb what he said.

And yet, in that excruciating moment, my thoughts went to Ronal Paul. "Does he know this? Have you told him this?"

"No," he said. "He's still in recovery."

Questions blurted out of my mouth before I had a chance to temper them. "Should we tell him? How should we act around him? Exactly what should I tell him?"

"Just love him," he said, his voice sounding heavy. "If you pray, I suggest you do that, but just be there to love and encourage him."

"Oh, Doctor," I said. "I believe in prayer." I noticed my left hand curled into a fist. Just moments before, I'd had peace. Now my worries wound as tight as my fingers pressing my palm. "Will you put him in ICU?" I asked.

171

"Not now, but in a moment's notice if necessary," he said. "I'll be up later to talk to you. Again, I'm so sorry."

I whispered a thank-you before hanging up. For a long time I sat on my son's bed as if frozen to it. I mulled over the doctor's words. No one at any time during his hospitalization mentioned that he might die. A few hours before, he had said he wanted to turn his life around. I prayed. Pleaded, really.

What's going on, God? How can this be? Is it true? Is my son going to die?

Even though my questions screamed at me, I felt calm. Maybe shock numbed me, but somehow I knew God gave me peace. I sensed his presence. From that point forward, God swooped me up and carried me.

I called Ronnie first. He answered in an upbeat mood—after all, just a few hours earlier Ronal Paul had owned up to his waywardness and decided to change. I had a hard time spitting out what the doctor told me. Finally I said, "The doctor doesn't think he will survive."

Ronnie said nothing. I had no words, either.

"I wasn't expecting that," Ronnie finally said.

"I know. Me, either."

"We'll be right up there."

"No," I said. "I'll be fine. You have already been here today. Ronal Paul will wonder why you're back. He doesn't know yet."

"What can we do?" he asked.

"Pray," I said.

"I love you. I'll talk to you soon."

"Okay, I love you, too," he said.

Ronnie didn't pray often, but I hoped he would if I asked, especially if he knew how important it was to me.

Next I called Linda. As I recounted my conversation with the doctor, Bret entered and sat down—so now I spoke to them both at the same time. I watched the pain in one friend's face and heard it in the other's voice.

The door opened, making way for Ronal Paul. I hung up the phone. Bret and I both took deep breaths, painting smiles on our faces. Before they situated him, Ronal Paul said, "I'm hungry."

"You are?" I asked.

"Yes. I want a Snuffers cheeseburger and cheddar fries. I feel great."

"You do?" Bret asked.

Ronal Paul nodded. "That doctor must've cleaned out my lungs because now I can breathe."

"Great," I said. "Snuffers it is. I'll call Wendi. She's coming to see you."

I stepped into the hall to call her from my cell phone. "I need you to stop by Snuffers on your way here. Ronal Paul wants a cheeseburger and cheddar fries."

"Really?"

"He's hungry, and he's asking for it."

At this point, she knew about the biopsy, but not the dire news. She agreed to grab what he wanted then hung up.

After Wendi arrived and Ronal Paul enjoyed his dinner, I asked her to step out in the hall. I recounted the doctor's conversation. I expected her to be surprised, but she wasn't at all.

"I can't believe he is that sick. Can you?"

She looked me square in the eyes and held both my hands. "Yes, Mom. I do believe he's *that* sick."

We paused in that position, holding hands, locking eyes.

She continued. "Are you going to be all right?"

"Yes." I knew as I spoke that word out loud that I'd be okay, no matter what happened. "I know God is in control. He's my strength," I said. "And he's prepared me for whatever happens. If he chooses to take him, then that is his will and he will get us through, right?"

"Right," she said.

As we waited for Dr. S., the infectious-disease doctor entered while Ronal Paul slept. "His condition is grave," he said.

I glanced over at my son, sleeping peacefully, thankful he didn't hear these words quite yet.

"I don't think he'll survive this, but we'll fight this pneumonia as aggressively as we can, to give him every chance." He looked at me.

I swallowed his news, but didn't respond.

"With a CD4 count of two, he'd have to really be a fighter."

In all our two-and-a-half weeks of Ronal Paul's hospitalization, we hadn't heard his CD4 count. Anything under 200 indicated full-blown AIDS. Two virtually meant a zero.

The doctor shifted on his feet. "Do you have DNR papers? We need to have this on file, if that's his wish, if a respirator becomes necessary."

I shook my head. I knew what "Do Not Resuscitate" meant. I had had this conversation with Mother's doctor shortly before her death.

"I don't recommend placing him on a respirator, as doing so would make things more difficult for everyone. It would only prolong the inevitable."

I nodded, then glanced at Bret and Wendi, trying not to cry.

"Would you like me to get them for you?" the doctor asked.

"Yes," I said.

He touched Ronal Paul's bed. "I'll do everything in my power to save his life." He left, while the gravity of the day sunk in.

Within five minutes, a staff member handed me the DNR papers. I looked them over but didn't feel comfortable talking about this with Ronal Paul after he woke up. I hoped they would not be needed just yet.

Around 10:00 P.M., Wendi noticed my fatigue.

"Go home, Mom. I'll wait for the doctor."

I didn't resist. I gave her a few questions to ask then said goodnight.

As I left my children there, I wondered if this would be the room where my son, Wendi's brother, would die. Only God knew.

Chapter 31

Last Days

For he loves us with unfailing love; the LORD's faithfulness endures forever. Praise the LORD!
—Psalm 117:2

The next day ticked off, slowly, painfully. Two days before Christmas. I called my cousin Larry on the way to the hospital, telling him the latest news through my tears.

"I just can't believe he's that sick. It's not possible."

"Brenda," Larry said, "I see this a lot as a pastor. It's called denial."

"I don't think I'm in denial," I said. "I can't see all the medical proof like the doctor can, but I see that Ronal Paul still has a good appetite. He's still alert. Still difficult to handle. How can the doctor be so sure of his condition?"

"Because he sees the situation with objective eyes," he told me.

I tried to believe his words. Then I asked, "Why can Wendi see that he is that sick when I can't?"

Larry laughed. "That's the definition of denial," he said. "Not being able to see reality."

I had to accept that I was in denial. I decided to make it a point of prayer.

Then I said, "Can you and Laura handle the service when the time comes?"

"Of course. Thanks for asking. You say the word, and we'll fly down."

As I neared the hospital, I prayed about my denial, then I thanked God that Bret lived so close and didn't have to work the month of December. Because of this, he could arrive early when Ronal Paul woke up, and I could take my time getting up and out the door. Besides that, Bret was like Ronal Paul's brother—closer than a friend.

That day several visitors came and left. Ronal Paul had a mediocre day—he didn't seem any worse, and he continued to be irritated at every little thing I did for him—normal for us.

As I watched him, I wondered about Christmas. How was I going to visit Ronal Paul and also have time with the rest of my family? Of course, I'd be next to him whenever necessary, but I did want to have Christmas with my daughter and her family. They planned to spend the night with me on Christmas Eve after we went to the candlelight service at church—just as they did every year. I thanked God that Shelley had finished my shopping for me while Natalie busied herself wrapping presents.

Still, I didn't know how I could be in two places at one time. Ronal Paul didn't want anyone to talk about Christmas because it saddened him to be in the hospital during this time of year. He didn't want any decorations in his room. For his sake, we avoided the subject and didn't wear Christmas-themed clothes. The last several Christmases had been difficult for all of us, he knew. But he did enjoy Christmas as a child, and he knew it was my favorite holiday. Perhaps this was part of his sadness. Anyway, I wondered how Christmas Eve and Christmas Day would work out. I'd just have to wait and see, taking each day one step at a time.

His strength slipped away later in the day. "Mom," he whispered. "I can't have any more visitors. Please." I called those who planned to come and let them know Ronal Paul's wishes.

I still hadn't broached the subject of the DNR papers in my purse. I couldn't do it yet. If I did, I'd be admitting the truth about his condition. Denial is a powerful thing! I hoped the papers wouldn't be necessary that night when I left for home. But as I drove away, my anxiety grew. I'd considered staying overnight, but if I did, I wouldn't rest well. I needed as much sleep as possible. My son didn't ask me to stay, but I sensed he didn't want me to leave either. I placed him in God's hands for the night.

Christmas Eve morning, the phone jarred me awake.

Oh no! No, please, God. No! Because of my bout with hearing loss, I'd been sleeping with my house phone and cell by my head for three weeks so I would hear any rings. I answered the house phone.

"Mom. I can't breathe. I need you," Ronal Paul said.

Relieved to hear his voice, I told him I'd get there as soon as I could. I jumped in the shower, washed my hair, then grabbed my makeup and headed to the hospital with no makeup and wet hair.

Though his breathing continued to be labored, he calmed down with me by his side. I fixed my hair and put on my makeup in the bathroom. While there, he said my name.

I walked to his bed and sat down. "I'm right here."

He looked at me and said, "Don't let them put me on a respirator." He said the words with calm, peace even. Since he always wore an oxygen mask, I often struggled to understand him, but this time his words were clear. "If they put me on a respirator," he said, "it means I'm going to die, right?"

I told myself to exude the peace my son had. "You are very sick. If you get well, you're going to have to fight really hard. But if they want to put you on a respirator then, yes, that means you're going to die. If you do not want a respirator, then you need to sign some papers I have here. Do you want to sign them now?"

"Yes," he said. I pulled the papers from my purse and showed him where to sign. He signed as best he could.

I put the papers away. I took his hand. "We know that God is in control. He loves you, and he will make that call, right?"

"I know. If he gets me through this I am going to be a saint."

I kissed him on the forehead and went back into the bathroom to finish my hair and makeup. I marveled at the way God had handled that difficult conversation. Neither one of us got emotional. We both acknowledged that a respirator meant death, and that death would be prolonged if we put him on a respirator. We agreed we didn't want that to happen, so he signed the papers. But most important: we agreed that God was in control and we would accept his will.

I still had to obtain two signatures from unrelated witnesses to complete the DNR papers. About an hour later, Indian visited. I called Indian my other brother, and he was a friend who excelled during hospital visits. He might not stay long, but he stopped long enough to show his support and offer his help. And he meant it—he would help in any way he could. As he started to leave, I grabbed the DNR papers and stepped into the hallway with him. I explained the situation and asked him to sign as a witness, which he did. "You know I love you all," he said. "I'm heartbroken all this is happening." He hugged me, squeezing tears out of both of us.

Just as he walked down the hall, Linda and her husband arrived. Linda made brownies for Ronal Paul, which he devoured. It amazed me that his appetite could be so good, but I also remembered the staff gave him meds to promote appetite.

While he finished off the tray of brownies, I asked her husband to step outside with me. He also agreed to sign the DNR papers. I marveled at God's perfect timing. He provided people to sign these difficult papers so quickly.

Diann arrived just as Linda and her husband said goodbye. They shared hugs and Christmas wishes with one another. Bret didn't visit that day. He'd spent time at his dad's house for Christmas Eve with his family.

As the day slipped away, Ronal Paul fought for each breath. I called Wendi and told her to go to the two o'clock candlelight Christmas Eve service without me, and to please drive to the hospital afterward. Diann and I called the nurses several times to ask if anything else could be done to ease his struggle to breathe. They told us they called Dr. S., awaiting his instructions.

At 3:00 that afternoon, a nurse entered the room. "Dr. S. directed us to take Ronal Paul to ICU so we can administer stronger medications."

Ronal Paul looked at me and gave me the thumbs-up signal—a sign he welcomed and needed relief. Diann and I followed as far as they would let us go. One nurse told us we could return at 4:00 for ICU visiting hours. I touched Ronal Paul and held his hand. "We'll be back as soon as we can."

We had something to eat in the cafeteria. It may sound strange, but I thanked God they took him to ICU. There he'd receive constant care, which freed me to see him only at certain times. I didn't have to carry the weight of feeling responsible for his well-being. Also, I could now spend time with Wendi and her family, and Ronnie and his family for Christmas—one of God's little Christmas gifts to me.

Wendi and Rex arrived as Diann and I headed back to ICU at 4:00 P.M. When we walked through the ICU's double doors, I heard Ronal Paul cry out in pain. Up until now, he hadn't experienced much pain—discomfort and panic from not being able to breathe, yes, but not pain. I hurried down the hall, looking into every room until I found him. A doctor stood over him, doing something to the upper right side of his ribcage. Blood ran down his chest to his stomach and onto the bed. A nurse stood on the other side of him, assisting the doctor.

Ronal Paul's face contorted.

I heard someone say, "That's his mom."

"That's my son. What's happening?" I asked.

Immediately the doctor left his side and ushered Wendi and me into the empty room next door. This was Dr. S., who I'd yet to meet in person. He said, "He is dying."

The room blurred slightly, but I hung on.

"I really hate to be so blunt, but it's true. We took another X-ray—his condition has worsened significantly since yesterday. After you visit with him, I'll show you the X-rays. We'll put him on morphine and a respirator and keep him comfortable."

I found my voice and told myself to keep it steady. "No respirator," I said. "He doesn't want a respirator." I pulled the papers from my purse. "Here, I have the DNR papers."

He looked them over. "Good," he said. "If I'd known you had these in place, I wouldn't have moved him to ICU. We would've started the morphine in his room and you could've stayed with him."

And yet, I knew God had a plan through all this. He had allowed this ICU stay so I could have the opportunity to be with Wendi and Ronnie and their families on Christmas Day.

"Again, I'm sorry." He said the words with much compassion.

"How long?" I asked.

"It could be tonight or a few more days," he said.

"Thank you," Wendi replied.

Diann and Rex waited in the hallway. We didn't have to explain what we'd been told. They knew. The nurse had finished the chest IV line when we entered.

182

As Wendi and I stood next to him, he spoke through his oxygen mask. "I'm so glad you're both here. I love you both so much."

He knew. He heard the mention of morphine and a respirator.

My throat locked up and burned with the strain of emotion. I told myself to speak. "I love you, Son. I could never have asked for a better son. I love you so much."

Wendi said, "You are the best Bubba in the world. I love you."

"Tell Lorenzo I love him. I am sorry I have to leave so soon," he said.

We all sobbed quietly—an obviously emotional scene, but we tried to focus on comforting him.

"Heaven will be beautiful, Ronal Paul," I said. "Everything beautiful you can imagine." I paused, regained composure. "We'll see you very soon. This isn't goodbye; it's see you later."

He drifted to sleep as the morphine worked its way through his system.

What happened?

This wasn't what I expected when they told me he'd be in ICU. I expected heavier sedation to help his anxiety. So he could relax. So he could breathe better. Not to be told, "He is dying" and to have to say goodbye to him. The circumstances of the day came too quickly. Questions churned inside me.

Are they sure he is dying?

Are they putting him on morphine too soon?

Or am I still in denial?

Wendi and I held hands, watching Ronal Paul while tears wet our faces. Rex and Diann entered by our sides.

Was he gone to sleep for good? Would he wake up again? I didn't have the strength to ask the nurse.

I left the room to see the X-rays with the doctor. I had a hard time concentrating as he explained Ronal Paul's diseased and shredded lungs.

I called Ronnie, Bret, Linda, and my cousin Larry.

The nurse asked me for some contact information. When I gave her Bret's name and phone number, I mentioned that he was Ron's best friend and also a minister.

"Oh, if he is Ron's minister, then he can come in at any time day or night."

What a blessing to know that. I thanked God that I mentioned Bret's minister status, since I hadn't realized ministers could have unlimited visitation. Bret loved that, and it gave me great comfort, also.

Just as Wendi and I went back into his room, he woke up. He looked at us, then looked around confused. "I thought I was dying."

We didn't know what to say. The look on his face and his words were almost comical. We looked to the nurse, hoping she could help us out with his question. She gently answered him with, "Mr. Rhodes, you are dying, but it's a process. We don't know exactly when it will happen, but we will keep you comfortable."

He slept again.

His room and the outer hallway filled up with family. Everyone came. I smiled to see Eva's two daughters, April and Shelley Dawn, and their husbands. Shelley Dawn and Ronal Paul had always shared a special friendship.

Indian and his wife, Pam, and their daughter, Kristin, came. Kristin is a beautiful young lady inside and out. She loved Ronal Paul with a sweet adoring heart. She had been one of the twelve I had asked to be at the intervention.

Ronal Paul drifted in and out as family and friends came in and out and spoke to him. Many expressed that they didn't know that his illness was so serious. I explained that I didn't know either, until a few days before. It was still hard for me to embrace the news.

His cousin Shelley later told me how she felt when she visited during that time. "His eyes were open, but he stared straight up at the ceiling. He looked dead already—white as a ghost with sunken eyes. I'd never seen someone look so bad and still be alive." She sat next to him, recounting childhood stories. "I thought he couldn't possibly get worse. While he blank-stared at the ceiling, I guessed he was begging God to take him."

She looked into his vacant eyes, wishing someone would put sunglasses on him or close his eyes. She tried to communicate with him, hoping he'd hear her words somehow through the stare. "You did not deserve this," she told him.

"My prayer for him," she said, "was for God to give my cousin a miracle or take him now. From that point on, that was my prayer."

Bret came in unexpectedly. He couldn't stay at his dad's knowing that Ron was in ICU and not expected to live more than a few days. After everyone left, Bret insisted I go home. "I'll stay," he said.

Since it was Christmas Eve and God had provided excellent twenty-four-hour care, and with his best friend at his side, I went home to be with Wendi and her family, who spent the night at my house.

As I lay in bed that night, I thought over God's surprising provisions. The peaceful DNR conversation, people signing the papers, the kind doctor, Bret's availability, medications to calm Ronal Paul down. On the eve of the birth of God's only Son, the Savior of the world, I knew God's heart overflowed love and compassion for a mother, a sister, a family, and for a young man who was dying as a result of his own disobedience. No greater love than this.

Christmas Day arrived. I woke up with the grandkids and tried to make the best of the morning. I thanked God that Wendi had arranged for her ex-husband Luis to visit with Ronal Paul that morning, giving them both some together time and me the freedom to stay with Wendi, Rex, and the kids. Luis later told me that some of Ronal Paul's words to him were, "Just for the record, I love ya, buddy."

Considering the circumstances, we celebrated Christmas as best we could.

The pending loss hung in the air, but in that we sensed God's love for us and shared our love for each other. We finished up sooner than usual, so we went to Ronnie and Eva's for gifts and brunch. Thankful to be with everyone, I still longed to be at the hospital. So after the visit, I left for Medical City.

The rest of Christmas day became a beautiful memory. Ronal Paul stayed alert, and he kept a good attitude. He enjoyed visits from special people God had placed in his life. I watched as loved ones and friends came at different times during the day— thankfully not too many at once. The way the visits staggered gave Ronal Paul periods of rest. Several people came in turmoil but left with healing. Eight years of fear and disappointments faded away, replaced by tears of love and forgiveness and peace.

To my surprise, God provided a way to make Christmas Eve and Christmas Day a time of rejoicing.

On Monday morning, December 26, the phone woke me up again. My first thought was, *Well, Lord, you got him through Christmas*. I felt sure the hospital was calling to say he was gone.

But when I answered, the voice on the phone was Ronal Paul's.

"Mom, where are you? I can't breathe!" He said the words with great difficulty.

I knew he couldn't have dialed the phone by himself, so I asked, "Is your nurse there? Let me talk to her."

"He's breaking through the morphine," she said. "When he wakes up he gets extremely anxious. He is now saying that he wants to be put on a respirator."

"No!" I said. "Do not put him on a respirator." I needed to ask her a difficult question. "He is dying, isn't he?"

"Yes," she said.

Still living in the land of denial, I had a hard time believing this. How could he have such times of strength? His appetite was still great. His voice remained strong even though he could barely breathe. But the nurse said yes, so it must be true.

"I'll be there as soon as I can."

"We're moving him to a private room so you can be with him twenty four hours. That way, when he wakes up, he'll have family nearby and won't get so anxious."

I called Bret as soon as I hung up, asking him to please go see Ronal Paul. Then I called Wendi. We got to the hospital in record time.

He remained agitated when we arrived, but they soon got him settled in a double room, with only one bed so there was a lot of space for family and friends. As we entered the room, I took note of the room number: 1606. *This is the room where my son will die,* I thought. I don't mean to sound morbid, but these are the thoughts of a mother having to let go of her child.

Bret went to Ronal Paul's house to pick up the Christmas gifts he had purchased for Wendi and me. Ronal Paul had told me several times during the last few months that I would love my Christmas present—the best he'd ever found.

I called Bret to give him the new room number. He told me Ronal Paul sent him to the house not just to pick up the presents but also to remove anything he wouldn't want me to see after he was gone. He was concerned that I would go to his house and see things that he had never intended for me to see. This must've been what he had on his mind when he woke up earlier and panicked. This touched me that he worried about such things, but I wanted him to relax and not worry.

It took Bret most of the day to accomplish his task, but when he returned with our gifts, Wendi and I were moved and pleased. Ronal Paul had picked out breathtaking wall tapestries for us. My tapestry was a beautiful staircase laden with flowers and vines pointing toward a wooden door, and Wendi's was a picturesque fountain. Both looked like scenes from my trip to Italy a few months earlier. He picked the colors perfectly, each matching our homes.

He told me exactly where he thought I should hang mine—and, of course, it was the perfect place. But while Ronal Paul was in the hospital we hung them up in his hospital room. While he slept, Bret, Wendi, and I created a twenty-four-hour schedule so he wouldn't be alone. Wendi would take the first shift from 8:00 A.M. to 4:00 P.M. I would be there 4:00 P.M. to midnight, and Bret would stay from midnight until 8:00 A.M. Bret went home to sleep for a while.

When Ronal Paul woke up, I told him about the schedule and that he would never be alone. Not for one minute.

"Until I die, right?"

I took a deep breath. "Yes, Son. Until you die."

He relaxed more after that short conversation.

We asked Ronal Paul if he wanted us to call Don, his ex-life partner of several years.

"Please," he said.

Don arrived within a few hours, glad that we'd called him.

Ronnie and Eva came by to visit. Ronal Paul tried to talk and listen as we all chatted about various things. At one point he looked at Ronnie. "Well, Uncle Ronnie, this is how I'm going out."

What a difficult statement to respond to! My heart went out to Ronnie, who cleared his throat and looked right at my son and said. "We're here for you, Ronal Paul."

Linda arrived with more brownies, and Ronal Paul inhaled them as quickly as he saw them.

During her visit, Wendi said, "I'd like to go with Rex to take Natalie to the airport." She looked at Linda. "Would you be willing to take half of my morning shift tomorrow from 8:00 until noon so I could go?"

"Of course. I'd be happy to," Linda said.

Before Wendi left, she reached into her purse to get a piece of gum. Ronal Paul heard the rustling of paper since he had special radar for anything smacking of food.

"What do you have?" he asked.

"Nothing." She dropped the gum back in her purse, knowing he couldn't have any. "Just getting the keys from my purse."

Awake, Ronal Paul wanted to eat. And eat.

By 10:00 P.M., I sat alone with him. Tired, I attempted to watch TV, holding his hand. Even though my body and heart ached, I had no doubt of God's control over the situation. He arranged for the ICU stay to last from Christmas Eve through Christmas Day. And now we'd created a good schedule so he wouldn't be alone. I marveled at God's love and faithfulness to us.

Ronal Paul interrupted my private reverie. "Mom, can you see that?"

"Can I see what?"

"God is rocking me in his hand. Can you see it?"

I smiled. "No, but that's wonderful. He loves you and wants you to rest." I continued to hold his hand as tears ran down my face. When Bret arrived at midnight, I kissed Ronal Paul goodnight. "I'll see you tomorrow afternoon," I said.

The next day, Tuesday, December 27, I spoke to Bret as soon as I woke up.

"They've increased his morphine levels," he said.

I knew what that meant.

"Brenda," he said. "He had an episode last night."

"What do you mean?" I asked.

"He got out of bed."

"He did? How could he do that?"

"I don't know," Bret said. "But he did. He said, 'I have to go.'"

"Where did he want to go?" I asked.

"He said he needed to go to the garden. Then he told me I'd have to help him up," Bret said. "But once he stood, he couldn't stay that way. He got back into bed. That's when I asked the nurse if we could up his morphine."

Once during the night, he told Bret, "Jesus has a hold of me."

"That's great to hear," Bret said.

"I can feel him holding me."

That night, while Ronal Paul and Bret spoke of heaven, the Lord moved Bret to start on his eulogy. Bret sat next to Ronal Paul, working on his laptop while Ronal Paul tried to rest.

He told Bret the same things he told me. "If I ever make it out, I'll never do drugs again. But I'm afraid I screwed it up," he said.

He and Bret prayed together before the nurse administered more morphine. "Ronal Paul knew Jesus' sacrifice and was ready to see him," Bret told me later.

"Lord," Bret prayed, "Give us both a fresh start. Forgive us both for the lifestyle we led. For the choices we've made. And forgive Ron right now."

Ronal Paul said "Amen." "Soon I will be free," he told Bret.

When the morphine lulled Ronal Paul to a peaceful sleep, Bret broke. "Please God," he cried, face to the floor. "Please, not Ron right now. No, God."

The Lord told him, "It is time." He took a deep breath, settled himself, then felt God's peace. That's when I called him.

"Is he all right?" I continued our conversation.

"He's now sleeping in what they told me is comfortable, constant sedation."

"Is he aware of anything ?"

"He can hear, but he can't respond. He'll have periods of sleep and wakefulness, but he can't open his eyes. The nursing staff told me this was all part of the process."

I hung up, my heart heavy.

Linda showed up for the morning shift. I called her during her stay. She watched over him beautifully, as I knew she would. She talked to him, prayed for him, and kept records of his vital signs.

"What's that noise?" I asked.

"He's moaning," she said. "The nurse said moaning was normal. Don't worry, he's comfortable."

I prayed that he was.

Linda stayed until Wendi arrived. I arrived early, about 2:30 P.M. Wendi visited until I sent her home. I could see when Ronal Paul woke up because he'd try to open his eyes, but only his eyebrows would raise. I had to know he was comfortable, that the moaning didn't mean he suffered. He couldn't move his hands or fingers to squeeze my hand, so I leaned over him and said, "Ronal Paul, I promised that you'd be comfortable. Raise your eyebrows if you are comfortable."

Slowly he raised his eyebrows. I thanked God through my tears.

Several friends and relatives visited again. Don, Ronal Paul's former life partner, returned. I was thankful we'd called him yesterday, since that was the last day Ronal Paul could speak.

My cousin Larry called to check on us. I brought him up to date on Ronal Paul's condition—the morphine, the diagnosis, his raised eyebrows.

"Is that Ronal Paul I hear in the background? The moaning?"

"Yes," I said.

He encouraged me, prayed for me, then said goodbye.

Later, Larry told me that when he heard him moaning he knew it wouldn't be long. As a minister, he'd been with many dying people. He knew what the moaning meant.

The internal medicine doctor returned. "I've stopped all antibiotics," he said. "There's no need for them any longer." He squeezed my shoulder. I could see compassion in his eyes.

Dr. S. entered and stood at the foot of Ronal Paul's bed. "This sucks," he said.

"Is that a term you learned in medical school?" I asked.

He smiled at my attempt at humor. He must've assumed I used laughter to cover up my pain. He paused then said, "Stay with him. Keep family with him."

"We're with him every minute." I looked at him "Thank you doesn't seem enough. But I really appreciate your care and compassion."

He nodded and left the room.

At midnight, I went home.

Chapter 32

Ronal Paul's
Last Day on Earth

For God has said, "I will never fail you. I will never
abandon you." So we can say with confidence, "The
LORD is my helper, so I will have no fear."
—Hebrews 13:5–6

On Wednesday, December 28, 2005, I called Wendi as
soon as I woke up.

"Shelley's with me," she said.

"Good. How is he doing?"

"He's about the same," Wendi said.

I hung up and then started looking for pictures to put on display at the funeral home, rummaging through boxes of memories. At that moment, the weight of Ronal Paul's impending
death hit me. As I looked at his sweet face as a baby, then as a
child growing up to a young man, I fell into a heap.

"Oh, God," I wept. "What happened to my son? How can this
be happening?" I couldn't believe that in that moment, I was
picking out pictures for my son's funeral. A mother shouldn't
have to do that. I didn't want to *have* to choose pictures. How

do you summarize a life in two dimensions like that? A freckled toddler laughing at the sunshine. A third-grade school picture, teeth missing. Ronal Paul at the age my husband molested him. The muscled twenty-something, handsome. It felt like too much. But I knew I had to finish, and I knew it was time to have a good cry. So I cried as much grief as I could muster while the silent house, full of memories, said nothing.

I called Wendi at noon.

"He's not moaning as loud," she said. " Shelley's holding his hand."

"What do the nurses say about less moaning?"

"They assured me he's comfortable. That this is part of the process."

I hung up. I could feel my pulse throughout my body. Oh, the grief! The loss. My son. My only son.

Later, Shelley and Wendi told me about their last moments with Ronal Paul.

"Since I didn't have anything going on that day," Shelley said, "I thought I'd go hang out with Wendi. Keep her company."

They both chattered about their lives as kids, told stories. "I held his hand on one side; she held his other hand. During our storytelling, I noticed Ronal Paul's pulse. You could see his heartbeat in his throat, throbbing fast. I wanted to ask the nurses, 'How long will this phase last?' But I didn't. I hoped maybe God would give him a miracle."

"We talked really loud. We asked him to raise his eyebrows if he heard us. He did," Shelley said.

Wendi recounted the last moments with her brother. "I'm not the sappiest person—it's my own way to protect my heart, I suppose. So I didn't leave with fanfare. I simply kissed him goodbye and said, 'I'll see you tomorrow.'"

I arrived at the hospital at 4:00 P.M. I could tell immediately the reason he didn't moan as loud was that he'd weakened significantly. Wendi and Shelley seemed tired. I hugged and kissed them, sending them home to their families.

In the emptiness of the room, the nurse slipped in.

"It won't be very long," he whispered.

"What do you mean by not very long?"

"Soon," he said.

I walked over to the side of the bed. I held my son's hand. "It's just you and me, buddy." His breathing changed in that moment. The moaning stopped, his breath shallow. He pulled in air in longer and longer intervals.

I could see, in that moment, that Ronal Paul had waited for me to arrive. Humbled, I thanked God for such a gift. My son may not have honored me the last years of his life when drugs stole his kindness, but he'd given me this one last act of honor.

I put my other hand on his chest, talking and praying him through to heaven.

"I love you," I said. "I'll miss you. You know that. But I need to let you know that it's okay to go now."

His breathing slowed.

"Whatever you see—a light, a hand, Jesus—whatever, it's okay to go on over."

No more moaning. Even slower breaths. He seemed to relax into the bed. I felt his warmth through his hand, his chest. That great heart kept its beating, giving life to my son.

"Dear Lord," I prayed. "I give you my son. Thank you for giving him to me. Now I give him back to you."

I looked up at the doorway. My nephew Eddie stood there. He knew what was happening. He'd been through the same rough situation with his grandfather two years before on Christmas day.

I motioned for him to wait a minute.

He nodded and stepped to the side of the door.

I wanted complete peace and calm to permeate the air around Ronal Paul and me. I promised him comfort, peace. And I would do anything I could to keep that promise until he took his last breath.

I continued talking to him and praying.

He did not struggle.

He did not move.

He did not open his eyes.

He slipped from me peacefully.

I stood in silence for a moment, awash in the grief-filled holy moment.

I composed myself, then called for Eddie. He stepped into the doorway.

"Go get his nurse, and call Wendi and Shelley. They just left."

The nurse arrived, listened for a heartbeat, then nodded. He left the room to call his supervisor.

Eddie returned to the room. I fell into his arms. We wept together. How perfect for God to send my nephew at this moment. I hadn't known he was coming, but I thanked God he stood there when I needed him.

All of a sudden Wendi ran so fast down the hall that she couldn't stop when she came to the door. She slid past and turned around, then entered the room, crying.

"Bubba, Bubba!" she wept. "I was here all day. You waited for Mom, didn't you?"

Later, Wendi shared with me how she felt in that moment. "I was mad," she said. "What's the deal with that? Why couldn't I have been with my brother when he died?" she asked.

But she said, "God knew I probably didn't need that experience. God made it clear that he was in control. He wanted my brother clean and sober so he could see Jesus more clearly. So that Ronal Paul could make the decision. He was spiritually prepared, now that he got sober. For the first time in a long time, he could see the big picture of the world, not just his own little world. He thought he could tell God how to do things. But in the end, he understood that he wasn't telling God anything."

While Wendi cried, I put my arm around her. "It was just as God planned," I said. "You were here with him all day, and I was with him when he died."

Then Shelley came in, disbelief on her face. "We were here all day. We just left!"

We all hugged and cried. How beautifully ironic that I wept with my kids—Wendi, my nephew Eddie, and my niece Shelley—while Ronal Paul left for heaven. God's love permeated the room.

Don, Ronal Paul's previous life partner, arrived soon after—I considered him one of my kids too. Immediately, Bret drove over after I called him. I called Ronnie. He and Eva were already on their way. Linda had started to go to a movie, but had decided to come to the hospital instead. God surrounded me with the exact people I would've hand picked to be there on that difficult day. He drew them from different parts of the Dallas area, all at the same time. I didn't have to worry. God knew who I wanted to be there and took care of it beautifully. He orchestrated everything.

As we walked out of the hospital, the most beautiful sunset greeted us. We all said, "Wow" at the same time. The sky boasted purples and blues and pinks, absolutely brilliant. I understood the sunset wasn't just for us, but I knew it was, in part, God's way of welcoming my creative and loving son to heaven.

Chapter 33

Grace Remembered

Then you will experience God's peace, which exceeds anything we can understand. His peace will guard your hearts and minds as you live in Christ Jesus.

—Philippians 4:7

Ronnie, Eva, and Wendi came with me to see the funeral director, helped me pick out the coffin, and made all the arrangements. We held visitation the night before the funeral. Bret and Don picked out the clothes Ronal Paul would be buried in on New Year's Eve, December 31, 2005.

As we rode to the church for the service, I felt complete peace. I knew beyond a shadow of a doubt that God was in control. After all, he had beautifully provided for us in the last month. I couldn't wait to see what he would do at Ronal Paul's funeral service.

We held the memorial service at my church's chapel, filled to capacity with many friends and family. Bobby was not able to attend, being incarcerated at the time.

Diann's husband sang Ronal Paul's favorite song, "In the Arms of an Angel" by Sarah McLachlan. Now, he truly mingled with angels. Larry conducted the service. He and his wife, Laura, sang while she played the piano.

When Bret rose to speak, my heart caught. Here was Ronal Paul's most faithful friend in the world, who had given his life back to God. Breathing proof that change was possible. There, confident and broken, he looked at me, then spoke.

> "When someone you love dies, you can't help but think whether or not they are going to heaven. I've had a few people question me on the state of Ron's soul. Personally I have no doubt I'll be seeing Ron in heaven. Jesus says in John 6:40, 'For my Father's will is that everyone who looks to the Son and believes in him shall have eternal life, and I will raise him up at the last day' (NIV).
>
> "I know from experience that Ron has looked to the Son of God and believed in him. One of the first real conversations Ron and I ever had was about God, and our belief in his Son Jesus. It's one of the many things that drew us close. I can remember on more than one occasion after being out we would bring a couple of people back to his condo, and we would wind up witnessing to them. It was like we were tag teaming for Christ.
>
> "Jesus also said in John 5:24, 'I tell you the truth, whoever hears my word and believes him who sent me has eternal life and will not be condemned. He has crossed over from death to life' (NIV). This verse tells us that for those who believe in Christ Jesus, death is simply a stepping-stone into our inheritance of eternal life.
>
> "Ephesians 1:13–14 says, 'And now you Gentiles have also heard the truth, the Good News that God saves you. And when you believed in

Christ, he identified you as his own by giving you
the Holy Spirit, whom he promised long ago. The
Spirit is God's guarantee that he will give us the
inheritance he promised and that he has purchased
us to be his own people. He did this so we would
praise and glorify him.'

"Ronal Paul was sealed by the Holy Spirit when
he was eight years old and, therefore, will not be
condemned, because he has the guarantee of an
inheritance in God's kingdom.

"Spending the past couple of weeks with him
in the hospital I had the opportunity to talk with
him and pray with him. I consider myself blessed
to have seen my best friend once again call on the
name of the Lord before he passed.

"I heard a story just last week about how Ron
was witnessing to a young lady and literally got
down on his knees and begged this young lady to
get on her knees with him and accept Jesus into
her life.

"In our eyes, the end of Ron's life might not
have completely reflected that of Christ's. But to a
good number of people lost in the darkness of this
world, Ron stood as a light. He was always willing
to go out of his way to help someone. It didn't matter what that person needed, Ron was there to help.
If someone needed a place to stay, no problem, you
could sleep on the couch. Need a hand moving?
Ron was right there. His generosity never changed.
His heart was always in the right place because his
heart belongs to Christ.

"Ron has on many occasions shown the love
of God in his actions; that is why so many people
were drawn to him. That's why I was drawn to him.
He knew how to truly show unselfish love toward
another person. That's how I will always remember

him—as a kind, generous, loving individual with a sincere concern for others' well-being."

Larry rose. He patted Bret on the back as he left the pulpit. They'd shared a long talk the night before about Bret's former life, his heart, and his love for Ronal Paul. Larry later told me that his friendship with Bret helped him have more empathy for men who struggle with homosexuality.

Larry extended his hand out to me. I walked up to the pulpit, holding my paper, praying for peace and a steady voice. The night Ronal Paul entered into heaven God had given me the words to say at this time. The words poured from his heart to my heart to the paper. It was with his supernatural strength that I shared in that moment.

"I just want to soak in all your faces for a few seconds—and say a quick prayer that I can get through this.

"I have heard people say that they can feel the prayers of others when they are going through a tough time. Well, now I know what they mean. Your love and prayers have been a great support for me and my family, not only during these last few weeks, but for the last several years as Ronal Paul struggled with life.

"I love each one of you dearly. I am overwhelmed by God's grace expressed through all of you. Thank you.

"Ronal Paul was a wonderful son for his first twenty-six years. I could not have asked for a more loving, supportive son. He saw me through many ups and downs. He was always there for me. His devotion was a great strength and blessing to me. We never doubted our love for one another. Our bond was very strong.

"As his life spiraled out of control, it was devastating, not only for me and Wendi, but for our whole family and close friends. It seemed that the more we tried to reach him, the further away he went. Almost everything he did for the last seven to eight years was life-threatening. It was awful to watch him self-destruct.

"I am so thankful that God rescued me on January 20, 1999, when I was at my lowest point of fear and helplessness. From that point on, I knew that I was going to be okay. But the storm still raged in Ronal Paul's life. He continued to make bad choices almost daily. I prayed every day for God to deliver him. And he did!

"But this is not what God wanted.

"This is not what I wanted.

"This is not what Wendi wanted.

"This is not what any of you wanted.

"But, obviously, it was the only way that God could deliver him.

"Ronal Paul belonged to God. He had accepted Jesus Christ as his Savior as a child. Even though he strayed from God's will and wandered away from God, God never left him. He loved him and eventually brought him back.

"Ronal Paul made peace with God this last week. He said he would totally change his life— even said he was going to be a 'saint'—if he got through this and had another chance. But God knew him better than he knew himself and chose to take him out of this world. Why? Because he loved Ronal Paul and knew what was best for him.

"Now he is safe.

"It is my hope and prayer that his life and struggles will be an example to every young person here. Unfortunately, a bad example. Stay close to God. Stay within his boundaries. He didn't set boundaries to spoil your fun, but to keep you safe because he loves you. Every one of you. He loves you and you and you.

"As we talk about choices, I am thankful that even though Ronal Paul made so many bad choices, he made the most important choice right. He chose Jesus.

"If anyone here does not know Jesus Christ as your personal Savior, I pray that you will before you walk out of here today.

"When you remember my son, please don't think of his many mistakes, but think of God's Son and his amazing grace."

Larry spoke about Jesus, his love, his sacrifice—for those left behind. "We can be reunited with loved ones," he said, "if we die in faith."

I remembered Wendi's recent words. "I'm happy that he's in heaven," she said. "Now he finally has time with Papaw. I can picture him so happy."

Larry continued, "Ronal Paul died a Christian because we're not Christians by what we do or don't do. It's what Jesus did. We all have habitual sins; we all struggle with them. And now he's free from that struggle."

Yes, God did indeed deliver him. My son is finally free. And in that, I rejoice.

Chapter 34

Life After Ronal Paul

But with God everything is possible.
—Matthew 19:26

Gaod has brought me much healing, but it's a struggle to deal with my own regret. I'm sure that is why I am a people pleaser—and an enabler—making up for my past. I love people almost too much. I can be possessive and jealous. I am afraid of losing the love of others. I hold on very tightly.

I'm heartbroken I let my father's death turn my heart away from my heavenly Father all those years. Oh, what heartache could've been spared had I turned to God instead of running one thousand miles the other way! I thank God he is compassionate and grace-filled. That he chose to rescue me on that car ride home, that he called me by name. I couldn't have endured Ronal Paul's waywardness without the Lord in my life. He knew that. Yet, it occurred to me recently that when God did rescue me, when he did call me by my name, he scolded me. "Brenda, let me be God. You be Brenda. Let me be God." I had not thought of myself as stubborn, but obviously I am, or was.

He had to let me think I had lost everything before he rescued me. Whatever it took, I am forever thankful.

I regret loving so much that I didn't discipline my children well. Being a young mother, I cherished their friendship over my responsibility as a parent. I confided in them too much, let my children do pretty much what they wanted. Sometimes I threw money their way, thinking that would prove my love. I wanted them to be happy, and I gave them what I thought they needed.

When Mother lived with us, I let her control me to the extent that I neglected my children when she called for me from her bedroom.

I regret not praying through my marital decisions. I wish I had stayed single after divorcing Bobby, at least until the kids were grown. I know each marriage negatively affected not only me, but my family, my children. Today I'm happily single, thankful God has stepped in as my husband.

I regret bailing Ronal Paul out too much. I did walk away more than once, but each time he got better I became too involved in his life, too soon. Detaching was really hard for me. Many times, without intending to, I enabled his bad behavior. I wish I hadn't.

And yet.

And yet . . .

Today, I still feel like a little girl most of the time. I am God's little girl. He rescued me, began a change in me that is still continuing, and made it possible for me to endure my son's death. I could not have done it without the steady love of my heavenly Father. He provided good friends, a great church, and a devoted family. He gave me his Word when I felt like giving up—always at the perfect time.

He has brought me through forgiveness. Jesus demands that we forgive; it is not an option. Matthew 6:14–15 says, "For if you forgive men when they sin against you, your heavenly

Father will also forgive you. But it you do not forgive men their sins, your Father will not forgive your sins." That is tough stuff. How could I ever forgive my second husband for what he did to my son? How can I forgive myself for dragging my kids through so many of my own bad decisions? Of course I never would have been able to forgive without God and the Holy Spirit.

My friend Linda does volunteer work for an organization called The Road Adventure. They hold seminars to help people work through past experiences that hold them back from being all they can be for themselves, their families, and God. It was there that I worked through forgiveness for Con and for myself. It wasn't easy, but I am now free of anger and vengeful thoughts toward Con. I am free—most of the time—from guilt for my past choices.

If you struggle from debilitating guilt and unforgiveness, I would strongly encourage you to contact The Road Adventure. You can get further information at www.theroadadventure.org. Linda sees miracles and lives changed every month.

I am living testimony of this verse: "He comforts us in all our troubles so that we can comfort others. When they are troubled, we will be able to give them the same comfort God has given us" (2 Cor. 1:4). This is the verse also used by the Stephen Ministry.

In every possible way, God rescued me. And comforted me. And gave me the privilege of comforting others.

I will rejoice every day of my life for his beautiful intervention.

Thank you for choosing to read my story. Remember, God does not have favorites. He loves us all the same. If your life is out of control, his arms are strong enough to hold you up no matter how heavy your burdens. His love is complete. He gave his life for you. His compassion will warm your heart and give you a peace that you never knew existed. Just reach up and take

Someone's Son
A mother's fight for her gay, drug addicted son

his hand. You will hear him say, "I will get you through. Hold on! I've got you."

He will never leave you or forsake you. Follow him and you'll never be alone again. This doesn't mean you'll never have troubles again, but it does mean that he will lead you through all of them.

The power of his love and faithfulness is amazing!

The next time you see or hear of someone like Ronal Paul, please remember:

He is not just an angry person struggling with life.

She is not just another homeless person.

He is not just another gay man.

She is not just another drug addict.

He is not just another AIDS patient.

He or she is someone's brother or sister, father or mother, friend, cousin, niece, or nephew.

She is someone's daughter.

He is *someone's son.*